THE SUNDAY TIMES

101
WAYS OF

SAVING
TAX

THE SUNDAY TELEGRAPH

101 WAYS OF SAVING TAX

BILL PACKER
△ Touche Ross

Pan Books
London, Sydney and Auckland

Acknowledgement

Bill Packer would like to record his thanks to Elaine Baker, whose original concept this book was and who contributed much of the initial material.

First published April 1982
Second edition, updated March 1983
Third edition, completely revised March 1984
Fourth edition, updated and revised March 1985
Fifth edition, updated and revised March 1986
Sixth edition, updated and revised March 1987
Seventh edition, updated and revised March 1988

This edition published 1990 by Pan Books Ltd
Cavaye Place, London SW10 9PG
in association with *The Sunday Telegraph*

9 8 7 6 5 4 3 2 1
ISBN 0 330 31701 6

Photoset by Parker Typesetting Service, Leicester
Printed and bound in Great Britain by
Richard Clay Ltd, Bungay, Suffolk

PREFACE

The 1990 Budget was a 'first' for two reasons. It was the first Budget for John Major, thrust into the hot seat after Nigel Lawson's resignation. It was also the first televised Budget. For 80 minutes, the new incumbent at Number 11 Downing Street endured the cameras to deliver the most difficult Budget since 1981. With the economy turning down, with inflation and the trade deficit uncomfortably high, Major had little room for manoeuvre. Taxation on the whole was marginally increased.

But the virtually neutral stance did not prevent big changes in the realms of savings, charity and taxation for women. So there is lots of meat on the bone for a clear and concise tax guide.

There is more need than ever today for good tax advice. Incentives for savings and investment are becoming increasingly substantial and complex. On top of the Business Expansion Scheme and the Personal Equity Plan, Major introduced Tessa, the Tax-Exempt Special Savings Account. The taxation position for married women has been transformed by independent taxation and the end of composite rate tax.

Unlike other tax books, this one, first published in 1982, shows you ways to cut your tax, not through complex schemes but by simple savings in areas often neglected even by financial sophisticates. It has been written as before by Bill Packer of Touche Ross, who has worked with great speed to incorporate all the changes of Major's Budget. Indeed his proofs had to be at the printers just a week after Budget Day.

John Jay,
City Editor, *The Sunday Telegraph*
March 1990

CONTENTS

The text includes the changes announced in the Budget on 20 March 1990. These may be amended before the 1990 Finance Act becomes law, probably at the end of July 1990. You should therefore check the position if you think you may be affected by the current Budget proposals.

1 BASIC QUESTIONS FOR THE INDIVIDUAL (Income Tax)

2 YOU HAVE EARNED IT (Taxation of the Employee)

3 NOW YOU ARE IN BUSINESS (Taxation of the Self-employed)

4 KEEPING GOOD COMPANY (Taxation of the Company – Corporation Tax)

5 SOME YOU WIN-SOME YOU LOSE (Capital Gains Tax and the individual)

1 BASIC QUESTIONS FOR THE INDIVIDUAL

INCOME TAX

1 Do I have to pay tax? If so, how much will I have to pay?

You may be amused to learn that, in theory, income tax is only a temporary measure; it has to be renewed by Parliament each year, and will cease to be imposed by Parliament when the country no longer requires revenue to be raised in this manner! Income tax was first introduced in 1799 to pay for the Napoleonic Wars, and was abolished after Waterloo, in 1816. In 1842, income tax was re-introduced by Sir Robert Peel, again as a temporary measure, but nearly a century and a half later income tax is still being paid! More recently, there have been suggestions that income tax will be unnecessary by the year 2000, but we will see!

As a starting point it is important that you understand what your *taxable income* is.

The total income of you, as an individual, should include your income from all sources whether earned or unearned. Up to 5 April 1990 where the taxpayer was a married man this was required to include his wife's income (see question 8); after that date the position has been radically changed so that husband and wife are now treated as separate persons for tax purposes (see question 9). *Earned income* is income arising from any office or employment, the personal carrying on of a trade, profession or vocation, pay or pension in respect of past services, and certain social security benefits. *Investment* (or *unearned*) *income* includes dividends plus tax credits, property income, interest from banks or building societies, annual payments, etc. (Note that these lists are not exhaustive.)

To arrive at your taxable income, from this total figure are deducted allowances, reliefs and charges on income (covered in later questions); the latter include annual payments and interest paid which are allowable for tax purposes. Charges are normally deducted from investment income first, unless it is more advantageous for you to have the deduction from your earned income.

Having arrived at the amount of your taxable income, this is taxed according to the income tax rates for that particular year. A year, for income tax purposes, commences on *6 April*, so the references to the end of a tax year are to *5 April*, not 31 December. Thus, the tax year 1989/90 runs from 6 April 1989 to 5 April 1990. The rates applied to your taxable income for both 1989/90 and 1990/91 are as follows:

Rate	Taxable income
%	£
25	1–20,700
40	over 20,700

The following example shows how the amount of taxable income is arrived at and how the tax is charged.

Example

Stan D. Easy is a retired army corporal aged 55 and in the year 1990/91 he receives an annual pension of £9,000; he is now in part-time employment and receives a salary of £12,000 per annum. He holds shares in various companies and during the year ended 5 April 1991 he receives dividends plus tax credits (see question 58) of £3,500. He pays mortgage interest on his house of £3,100, and he is a married man; his wife is 53. His taxable income for 1990/91 was as follows.

	£
Salary	12,000
Pension	9,000
Dividends + tax credits	3,500
Total income	24,500
less interest paid	3,100
	21,400
less personal allowance (see question 7)	(3,005)
married couple's allowance (see question 9)	(1,720)
Taxable income	£16,675

This is charged to tax at 25%: £16,675 at 25% = £4,168.75 and this is Stan's total tax bill. From this figure is deducted all the tax he has already paid and it is then possible to see whether he has paid too much or too little tax during the year, the balance being either collected from him or repaid to him (see also question 2).

2   When and how do I pay tax?

Tax will be collected from you in one of two ways – either by *deduction at source* or by way of an *assessment* issued by the Inspector of Taxes which informs you of the amount to pay direct to the Revenue.

The most common example of tax being deducted at source is if you are an employee – you will receive your weekly/monthly salary after tax and national insurance contributions have been deducted under the PAYE scheme (see also question 27). On the other hand if you are self-employed there is no employer to deduct tax from your earnings during the tax year. Instead, you will send in accounts each year to the Inspector of Taxes showing details of your income and expenditure for the year, he will then issue an assessment on your taxable profit for the relevant tax year (see also questions 36 to 51). Unearned income is also taxed by assessment unless it is a very small amount, in which case part of your personal allowances will be used to cover the amount chargeable.

There is yet another form of assessment to collect higher rate tax due on investment income. Generally, investment income is paid with income tax at the basic rate deducted or treated as deducted at source. If therefore you are liable to tax at a higher rate it will be necessary for the Inspector of Taxes to issue a special assessment (known as a 'taxed income' assessment) to collect the additional liability. This additional tax is not due for payment until 1 December following the end of the year of assessment concerned or 30 days after the date of issue of the assessment, whichever is the later; thus the additional liability for the year 1989/90 will not be due for payment until 1 December 1990 at the earliest.

Finally, even if you are an employee you may receive an assessment (which will show income from employment and the tax deducted) after the end of the tax year if, for some reason, you have paid too much or too little tax, despite the regular PAYE deductions made by your employer (see question 28 for more details).

For whatever reason you receive an assessment you should always check to see if it is correct. If you have a professional adviser you should authorise him to receive a copy of all assessments issued to you. In case the copy does not reach your adviser, you should give him your own copy of the notice of assessment as soon as possible.

3 What do I do if I do not agree with the amount of tax I am being asked to pay?

If you do not agree with the figures shown on the assessment you have 30 days in which to *appeal* against it, stating your reasons and whether or not you wish part, or all, of the tax charged to be withheld from collection until the figures have been agreed. The procedure for making an appeal or a request for postponement of the tax charged is covered in the notes which are always issued with a notice of assessment, but if you have a professional adviser he will deal with this for you.

If you appeal against an assessment on the grounds that it is estimated and the Inspector of Taxes is awaiting accounts or other details from you, you should not delay sending him the information. Indeed, should you fail to do this, he has the right to take you before an independent body called the General Commissioners who, when the facts are put before them, have the power to determine (or confirm) the assessment in whatever amount they consider appropriate. This could well lead to excessive tax having to be paid by you!

If you are self-employed you will normally pay the tax due in two equal instalments on *1 January* during the year of assessment and *1 July* immediately following the year of assessment. For the year 1990/91 tax is payable on 1 January 1991 and 1 July 1991 (remembering that the year commences on 6 April 1990 and ends on 5 April 1991). If the assessment is issued too late to pay tax on these dates you will be given *30 days* to pay the tax.

4 When should I send in my income tax return?

Strictly speaking, an individual is required to send in his return of income within 30 days of its date of issue (which is normally soon after the end of the tax year concerned). In practice, this time limit is not applied and the Inland Revenue will not normally take any action provided that the delay in filing the return is not, in their terms, *substantial*.

What constitutes 'substantial' in this context depends very much on the type of income involved and whether there is tax to pay by direct assessment on the individual or whether it is dealt with by deduction at source, e.g. under PAYE (see question 2). In particular, the Inland Revenue will expect a return to be made by *31 October* following the end of the tax year concerned where any of the following categories are involved:

(1) Where there is a new source of income;
(2) Where an estimated assessment has been made against income arising on an existing, known source of income, and although it was realised by the taxpayer that the amount assessed to tax was too low, no appeal was made against it.
(3) Capital gains.

Where this time limit is not met, or where in any other circumstances the Revenue consider that the delay in filing the return is substantial, they will normally seek to charge interest (currently at 13% per annum) on the tax payment which is in arrears as a result of this delay, and, in certain circumstances, penalties as well. These additional charges can commonly be avoided if the taxpayer supplies sufficient information to enable accurate (or at least reasonably accurate) assessments to be made on a timely basis; again this usually means supplying the required information by 31 October as before.

5   If I delay paying the tax due, am I liable to interest?

If there is tax to pay on an assessment, *the notice will always state quite clearly the due date for payment of the tax*. Remember there is an *interest charge* (currently at 13% per annum) which accrues daily from what is called the *reckonable date* (which will vary depending upon the circumstances) to the date payment of the tax is paid.

You should not delay paying your tax after the due and payable date: it will benefit no one, for you always run the risk of having an extra charge to pay: interest. If you incur an interest charge on overdue tax (of any description) it is not deductible for any tax purposes.

On the other hand, if the situation is reversed and the Inland

Revenue owe you a refund of tax, there may be a *repayment supplement* due to you. Again, this is calculated at 13% per annum and will be paid to you provided certain tests concerning the original due date of payment of the tax are fulfilled.

There is one other area which concerns collection of tax. In 1971 the Revenue introduced a practice whereby they would not collect arrears of tax if this had arisen due to some error on their part involving failure to make proper and timely use of information relating to a taxpayer's income or personal circumstances.

With effect from 14 March 1990, the proportion of arrears forgiven in this way depends on the taxpayer's gross income and ranges from all the tax being forgiven if the gross income is less than £12,000 to all the arrears being collected if the income exceeds £32,000. These limits apply separately to husband and wife from 6 April 1990, and are increased by £3,300 for pensioners. Prior to 14 March 1990, lower limits of arrears applied, determined by reference to the joint income of husband and wife if applicable.

These cases are very uncommon and the Revenue looks at the circumstances very carefully before a case of 'official error' is admitted.

6 Can I save tax by keeping quiet?

Many people think that if they do not send in their income tax returns or accounts it will save them tax. There are also a number of people who omit, quite inadvertently, to make entries on their returns of income or neglect to keep the Revenue informed of their circumstances. Finally, there are people who deliberately withhold information from the Inland Revenue in the belief that no one will ever know and they have therefore 'got away with it'!

These people are, of course, quite wrong in their views – there is no excuse for withholding details of your income and gains from the Inland Revenue. Even if the Inspector fails to send you an income tax return for completion, this does not discharge you from your liability – you should inform him even if he does not ask. Be certain you are not misled into thinking 'the Inspector will never know' – the Revenue has extensive powers which are used to obtain information not only from you as an individual, but from many other sources.

The most common source from which the revenue receives

information is the banks and building societies which, by law, have to forward to the Revenue, details of interest credited to each person's account where this exceeds a specified amount. This information is imparted to the individual's own tax office and checked with his return ... the rest is obvious! In many larger cases of omissions from returns, etc. there can also be *interest charges* and *penalties* levied in addition to the tax charged. The Revenue are becoming increasingly strict in this area and often go back a number of years in their investigations.

The answer to this question, then, is most definitely – no. Instead of paying *less* tax you *may end up paying large amounts in tax, penalties, interest* and possibly a *professional adviser's fees* incurred to help clear up the problem.

7 What is the basic personal allowance?

For 1989/90 the *lower* personal allowance was £2,785; for 1990/91 it is £3,005. This will be granted if you are an unmarried person (whether single, divorced or widowed), and even if you are not entitled to claim any other allowances, this amount will be deducted from your income before the tax is calculated.

Legislation was introduced in 1980 for indexation of the main personal allowances (including this relief) so the amount of relief should be revised each tax year, by reference to any increase in the retail prices index (RPI) during the 12 months to the previous December. There is also power to increase these allowances by a greater or lesser amount than the RPI, or even not to increase them at all.

8 I am married. What was the tax position of my wife and myself up to 5 April 1990?

As a general proposition, where a married woman was living with her husband or was wholly maintained by him, the husband was entitled to a higher personal allowance (*the married man's allowance*) amounting to £4,375 in 1989/90. (It should be noted that the status of the common law wife is not recognised for these purposes.)

In addition, the wife's income was treated for tax purposes as if it were her husband's; the husband was generally responsible for reporting his wife's income on his tax return and for paying the tax on it. It followed that the wife did not have any right of confidentiality in relation to her tax affairs.

This principle was, however, modified in certain circumstances:

(1) *Where the wife was working*. In this case the husband was entitled to an extra allowance, known as the *wife's earned income allowance*. This was the same as the single person's allowance as in question 7 (ie £2,785 for 1989/90) and was set against her earned income only. Thus if the wife was employed it was normally given in her PAYE coding (see questions 27 and 33); if she was self-employed it was given in the appropriate assessment. If the wife had only investment income, no allowance was given to her and the income was assessed to tax on the husband.

If the wife's earnings were below the amount of the allowance the excess was lost. However, if the husband's income was less than his total allowances, the wife could claim the balance of his allowances against her earned income. Thus allowances could pass from husband to wife but not the other way.

If the wife's earnings exceeded the allowances the balance was again taxed as part of the husband's income, possibly at a higher rate if this was appropriate. However, it was possible for husband and wife to elect jointly to have the wife's earnings taxed separately; this arrangement was known as the *wife's earnings election* and worked as follows. The husband continued to be assessed on his own earnings and on his wife's investment income but he only received the single person's allowance. The wife was also taxed as a single person, receiving the corresponding allowance, but in this way both parties received the benefit of their own basic rate bands.

The election had to be made jointly by husband and wife not later than 12 months after the end of the tax year for which it is to apply. Thus an election for 1989/90 could still be made up to 5 April 1991. It was certainly worth considering if the joint earnings were more than £30,511 in that year.

Example

Paul Over, a director of a knitwear manufacturing company, received a salary of £35,000 in 1989/90. His wife Eileen, a keep-fit instructress, earned £14,000 in that year.

Without the wife's earnings election tax was due as follows

	Total £	Paul £	Eileen £
Earnings	49,000	35,000	14,000
Less allowances:			
married man's allowance	(4,375)	(4,375)	
wife's earned income allowance	(2,785)		(2,785)
	£41,840	£30,625	£11,215
Chargeable to tax:			
at 25%	20,700	20,700	
at 40%	21,140	9,925	11,215
	£41,840	£30,625	£11,215
Tax payable	£13,631	£ 9,145	£ 4,486

With the wife's earning election tax was due as follows

	£	£	£
Earnings	49,000	35,000	14,000
Less single person's allowance	(5,570)	(2,785)	(2,785)
	£43,430	£32,215	£11,215
Chargeable to tax:			
at 25%	31,915	20,700	11,215
at 40%	11,515	11,515	
	£43,430	£32,215	£11,215
Tax payable	£12,585	£ 9,781	£ 2,804
Overall tax saving	£ 1,046		

(2) *Where husband or wife elect to have their income separately assessed*. This provided a means by which each party made a separate return of income and each accounted for the tax due on that income.

   However, it did not lead to any reduction in the overall tax liability of the couple.

9 How are my wife and I treated for tax purposes from 6 April 1990 onwards?

From this date, husband and wife are each to be treated as a separate individual for income tax purposes. Each is now entitled to a single personal allowance (as in question 7) and each will be charged separately to tax at the basic and higher rates as applicable; this arrangement is referred to as *independent taxation*. In addition there is a *married couple's allowance* which replaces the difference between the present single person's and married man's allowances: for the year 1990/91 this has been fixed at £1,720; if it had applied in 1989/90, this would have been £1,590 (4,375−2,785). In the first instance this allowance goes to the husband so that he will effectively be taxed in the same way as at present; if, however, he does not have sufficient income to make full use of this allowance any unused amount will be transferable to his wife. This facility does not apply to the single person's allowance of either husband or wife.

Applying this new basis to the example looked at above for Paul and Eileen Over, their joint tax bill for 1990/91 would be as follows:

	Total £	Paul £	Eileen £
Earnings	49,000	35,000	14,000
Less allowances:			
single person's allowance	(6,010)	(3,005)	(3,005)
married couple's allowance	(1,720)	(1,720)	
	£41,270	£30,275	£10,995
Chargeable to tax:			
at 25%	31,695	20,700	10,995
at 40%	9,575	9,575	
	£41,270	£30,275	£10,995
Tax payable	£11,754	£ 9,005	£ 2,749

It is particularly significant that exactly the same result would be achieved if the whole of Eileen's income had been investment income instead of earnings.

Husband and wife will now be responsible for making their own tax returns and for paying their own tax liabilities. It also means that the wife will now be able to maintain total privacy in dealing with her own tax affairs.

10 How can we as a married couple take advantage of the independent taxation arrangements described in question 9?

It will be appreciated that if the wife has no income, the benefit of her single person's allowance is lost. In these circumstances, the couple may wish to consider ways in which this situation could be rectified. If the husband's income wholly or very largely comes from his employment, there is probably very little that can be done (unless his employer supports job-sharing!)

Where, however, the husband is self-employed, there may be some scope for transferring income. For example, it may be possible for him to pay his wife a salary for helping to run the business, perhaps by part-time secretarial work. Commonly this has been set at a level equivalent to the wife's earned income allowance or to the slightly lower threshold for the payment of class 1 national insurance contributions (see question 17). It may now be appropriate to consider raising this significantly if the husband's profits are taxed at 40%.

However, it is important that the level of salary can be justified on commercial grounds, i.e. that it is at the same level as would be paid to an independent employee doing this job; if the Revenue considers the amount to be excessive under this test, they will disallow the excess in arriving at the husband's taxable profits, which would rather defeat the object of the exercise!

As an alternative, husband and wife may consider going into partnership together. Where the wife has a genuine power to enter into contracts on behalf of the partnership and shares in the business risks with the other partners, it would be difficult for the Revenue to argue that she is not a partner and hence to challenge the share of the profits that she receives; the 'commercial' test described previously is not applicable here. It is in order for partners to agree to split their profits between them in one way but to arrange their voting rights and interests in partnership assets differently.

Where the husband is the proprietor of a limited company, it may be possible for the wife to become an employee, perhaps a director, and be paid a salary accordingly. Here, again, this will have to be at a commercially supportable level. Alternatively, she could be given investment income by issuing her with shares on which dividends could be paid. These could be ordinary shares or, if preferred, shares of a special class carrying a right to dividend but with no voting rights or significant entitlement to assets on a liquidation.

Where the husband has substantial investments of his own, he may like to consider transferring some of these to his wife so as to provide her with investment income. Such planning may have considerable non-tax implications: for example, if it is wished to provide the wife with enough investment income to take her up to the edge of the 40% band, it would be necessary to give her an income of about £24,000 a year, which might well require the passing over of investments of the order of £240,000. In making any such arrangement, there is nothing to be gained by making gifts with strings attached or using complicated trusts. There is a specific anti-avoidance provision which will disregard for tax purposes any purported gift of income unless there is also a gift of the underlying capital (though this does not apply to partnerships).

Where assets are held in joint names, each spouse is automatically taxed on half the income unless a joint declaration defining a different split of their interests is made. Again, income and capital must be split in the same proportions. A declaration along these lines is not normally possible in the case of bank or building society accounts in joint names.

In any case, care should be taken to ensure that if the wife receives investment income which has suffered tax at source (as would generally be the case) she can recover such tax against her personal allowance. Thus bank or building society accounts which are subject to the composite rate tax system (see question 22) should, for the present, be avoided.

Finally, it should be noted that a married woman who receives a state pension on her account based on her husband's contributions will be taxed on the additional element and so will be able to use her own personal allowance against it.

● **11 What happens to my tax in the year of my marriage?**

Up to 5 April 1990

Husband: The *married man's allowance* is reduced by 1/12th of the difference between the single and married man's allowances, for each month in the tax year which ended before the date of marriage (i.e. ending 5 May, 5 June, etc.).

Wife: The single person's allowance is given throughout the year of marriage and the wife is not treated as married until 6 April following the date of marriage (i.e. the start of the new tax year). At this point the wife's personal allowances disappear, although if she is working it is replaced by the *wife's earned income allowance* (see question 8).

From 6 April 1990 onwards

Husband: In this case the married couple's allowance (see question 9) is reduced by 1/12th for each month in the tax year ending before the date of marriage (i.e. ending 5 May, 5 June, etc.).

Wife: She will be treated as a single person throughout the year of marriage and will be entitled to one single person's allowance in that year (and of course in succeeding years).

12 Are there any other allowances that I can claim for myself or my family?

Tax allowances in respect of children were generally abolished some years ago (but see question 15 – single parent families). The allowances have been replaced by child benefits which are payable direct to the mother of the child by the Department of Social Security normally through a post office or by credit transfer. These child benefits are not taxable.

There were a number of minor personal allowances which were available for years up to and including 1987/88 but which were withdrawn with effect from 6 April 1988. These were as follows for 1987/88:

dependent relative	
normal relief	£100
for certain single women	£145
daughter's or son's services	£ 55
housekeeper	£100

Detailed rules apply in determining one's eligibility for any of these allowances; if you consider that you may qualify, you should contact your Inspector of Taxes and explain the circumstances to him. Claims may be made up to six years back, i.e. to 1984/85 at the earliest.

In addition the following reliefs should be noted:

Blind person's relief: This can be claimed by a single person or a married man if he (or his wife) is registered blind throughout the whole or part of the year. If both spouses are blind, the allowance is given twice. Currently the allowance is £1,080 a year (1989/90: £540).

Life assurance relief: For most life assurance policies issued up to and including 13 March 1984, income tax relief at 12½% is allowed on the premiums paid. Normally the relief is given by means of a deduction by the payer from the premiums he pays, so that no intervention is required by the tax office.

The relief is not given on policies issued after 13 March 1984; it will also be withdrawn on any existing policies made before that date if the policy terms are altered so as to improve the benefits received.

Private health insurance: With effect from 6 April 1990, it is now possible in certain circumstances to obtain income tax relief on private health insurance premiums. The relief is available to a UK resident who pays premiums on a private health insurance contract on or after 6 April 1990, irrespective of when the policy was first taken out.

The person insured by the policy must be resident in the UK and must be 60 or over, except that in the case of a policy covering a married couple only one spouse has to be of that age. It should be noted that the person paying the premium (and so claiming the relief) need not be the person insured. Thus it is possible, for example, for an individual below the age of 60 to take out such a policy for the benefit of his elderly parents and obtain the corresponding tax relief on the premiums he pays.

The relief is intended to cover a comprehensive range of treatments, so as to include 'medical and surgical procedures (including diagnosis), the purpose of which is the relief of illness or injury, given or personally controlled by a registered medical or dental practitioner in the UK', together with most charges and fees consequent upon such procedures. The relief does not cover procedures such as 'alternative' medicine, dental treatment carried out in a general dental practice, general ophthalmic procedures not carried out in a hospital nor does it extend to cash benefits, i.e. to cover loss of earnings, except sums of up to £5 a night during private in-patient treatment. It is important to make sure that the policy does meet the various conditions laid down so as to establish that relief is properly due.

Tax relief is normally given by an arrangement similar to the MIRAS scheme for mortgage interest described in question 20, whereby the payer withholds income tax at the basic rate (currently 25%) from his premium payments and pays over only the net amount to the provider of the insurance. If he is a basic rate taxpayer no further relief is due to him, if he is liable to tax at a higher rate the additional relief is given by way of an adjustment to his PAYE coding or if he is not in employment in his tax assessment.

13 What happens if our marriage comes to an end?

For income tax purposes there are three ways in which a marriage can come to an end: *separation, divorce* or *death*. Technically the marriage is said to have ended when the parties 'cease living together' as man and wife. Separation can be formalised by a court order or by deed, but the term also covers the situation where the couple have separated in such circumstances that the separation is likely to be permanent, in which case a formal judicial separation order is not required.

If your marriage should come to an end, it will have the following effect on your income tax.

Husband: You are entitled to the married man's allowance (up to 1989/90) or the married couple's allowance (from 1990/91 onwards) for the whole of the tax year in which the marriage comes to an end (it is not apportioned as in the year of marriage); from the following 6 April you will be taxed as a single man.

Wife: If the marriage came to an end prior to 5 April 1990, your tax affairs would have been split between the two parts of the tax year before and after the date of separation or death. In the earlier period you would have been able to claim the wife's earned income allowance (if applicable) and wife's earnings election (see question 8), but generally your income would have been treated as part of your husband's in the usual way. For the later period you would have been taxed as a single person, being given the single person's allowance; in case of death, see also question 14.

Where the marriage comes to an end on or after 6 April 1990, you are treated as a single person throughout the year and will be entitled to the single person's allowance accordingly.

If the marriage has ended through separation or divorce it is quite likely that there will be some provision for maintenance to be paid by the husband in respect of his wife, or their children, or both. It may be that the separation is amicable, in which case the husband may be making voluntary payments to maintain the family. If he, during the period of separation, is considered by the Revenue to be wholly maintaining his wife (taking into account any other income she receives) he will continue to be given the married man's personal allowance. If this is the case, the voluntary payments are not treated as the wife's income for tax purposes.

For payments under a court order made before 15 March 1988 it is normally possible to treat them as a deduction for tax purposes from the payer's income and as taxable income in the hands of the recipient. In this connection it is important to distinguish between:

(1) income under a court order made in favour of the wife, which is her income;

(2) income under an order for the payments to be made to the wife (or any other person) for the maintenance of the children, which is also the recipient's income;

(3) income under an order made in favour of the children direct, which is then their income.

If the payments are made direct to the children, each child will be granted the single person's allowance.

For pre-15 March 1988 arrangements, in the tax year 1988/89 the recipient was not taxable on the first £1,490. With effect from 6 April 1989, the available tax relief to the payer is 'pegged'; the amount deductible by him will be limited to the amount deductible in 1988/89 and the amount taxable in the hands of the recipient is likewise limited to that taxable in 1988/89. Thus any upwards variations to pre-15 March 1988 arrangements do not have any tax consequences.

As regards court order or agreed maintenance payments made under arrangements entered into on or after 15 March 1988, these will generally be outside the scope of the tax system. The recipient of such payments will not be taxable on them and the payer will obtain relief only on payments up to the level of the married couple's allowance (£1,720 in 1990/91: see question 9) and then only until the recipient remarries.

However the previous rules will also apply to payments made under a court order applied for prior to 15 March 1988 provided that the order was made by the court by 30 June 1988.

From 6 April 1989 onwards, all payments, whether under the old rules or the new, are made gross.

14 What happens when I die?

When you die, if there is outstanding income tax to pay this liability will have to be met by your personal representatives, i.e. your executor or whoever is responsible for administering your estate. The implications for capital gains tax and inheritance tax are dealt with in Chapters 5 and 6 respectively.

If you are married the tax position depends on which spouse dies first. If the wife dies first, the husband will still be entitled to claim the married man's personal allowance or the married couple's allowance, as the case may be (see questions 8 and 9), for the whole of the tax year, and from the start of the next tax year he will be taxed as a single person. It is possible for the husband (or his executors) to disclaim responsibility for the wife's share of tax outstanding at her death where this would otherwise be his liability (see question 8), provided due notice is given to the Inland Revenue, normally within two months of the grant of probate.

If it is the husband who dies first, *prior to 6 April 1990* the wife's income from the beginning of the tax year to the date of his death would have been included in his final assessment to tax. She would then have been treated as a single person for the remainder of that tax year and subsequent years, being given the single personal allowance (see question 7) against her income which presumably will include a state widow's pension. Where the husband's death takes place *after 5 April 1990*, the widow will already have been recognised for tax purposes as a single person (see question 9) and her husband's death will not affect this aspect of her tax status at all.

In addition, a *widow's bereavement allowance* may also be claimed by the widow for the year in which her husband dies. The relief is available against her income following his death and is the same as the married couple's allowance (£1,720 for 1990/91; for earlier years, it was the difference between the single person's and married man's allowances, e.g. £1,590 in 1989/90). The allowance may be claimed if the husband was 'entitled' to the married person's allowance, even if the allowance had actually been foregone due to a wife's earnings election being in force, or to the married couple's allowance. The allowance is also available in the tax year following that in which the husband died, provided that the widow has not remarried before the beginning of that later tax year.

15 If I am the head of a single parent family what can I claim?

There is an additional allowance which may be claimed if you are a person (either male or female) who is not entitled to the married man's allowance, but you have children in your care. The amount of the allowance is £1,590 for 1989/90 and £1,720 for 1990/91; this is given *once only* irrespective of the number of children involved. If the allowance is being claimed following separation or divorce and both parents claim they are maintaining the children the allowance can be apportioned between them; if each parent is separately maintaining one or more of the children, each may be able to claim an allowance. The child must be resident with the claimant during the whole or part of the tax year; in addition, the child must be also be a child of the claimant or if not, must be under 18 and maintained for the whole or part of the year at the claimant's expense. In any event the child must be born during the year of assessment or be under 16 at the commencement of the year of assessment; alternatively, the child may be over 16 and undergoing full-time instruction at a recognised educational establishment, or undergoing training by an employer, for not less than two years, for a trade, profession or vocation.

This allowance may also be claimed by a married man whose wife is totally incapacitated (physically or mentally) throughout the year.

16 How can I prepare for my retirement?

During your working life you will pay national insurance contributions under a particular class (depending on whether you are an employee or self-employed), in the amounts laid down by the state. (See question 17 for more details regarding the various classes and amounts to be paid.) If you pay the full contributions for at least nine-tenths of your working life you will qualify for the full *basic retirement pension*. A woman entitled to a pension in her own right will normally receive it at the age of 60; a man at the age of 65. A married man will receive an additional amount for his wife but if she is entitled to a pension in respect of both her own and her husband's contributions, she may claim whichever is the higher pension.

In addition to paying national insurance contributions, if you an employee you may also be paying into a pension scheme. There is the *state earnings-related pension scheme (SERPS)* operated by the government, and since 1978 every employer has had to pay into the state scheme for all his employees unless he is running an *approved* private scheme in which case he can *contract out*.

If your employer has contracted out this will not affect your entitlement to the basic national insurance retirement pension or to any other social security benefits.

Your employer may be running his scheme in-house or through a life assurance company, but irrespective of who is running the scheme, it *must be approved* by the Inland Revenue Superannuation Funds Office and by the Occupational Pensions Board.

The state scheme offers a considerable improvement on the terms of many pension schemes that were being run before 1978, with the benefits increasing in line with the increases in the RPI; however, there are still a number of disadvantages that the state scheme has compared with an occupational scheme that has been duly approved. There can be no flexibility on the age of retirement, nor can a tax-free lump sum be paid at retirement; there is generally no income tax relief for the individual's payments into the scheme, and earnings over £16,900 for 1989/90 and £18,200 for 1990/91 are unpensionable.

Increasing concern has been expressed in recent years about the provision of pensions for individuals in employment, in that *occupational pension schemes* (i.e. those organised by employers) tend to provide the best benefit to *long serving* employees. Generally, they work to the disadvantage of employees who change jobs, particularly those who move into a new job near (perhaps within five years of) retirement. Mobility of employment of this kind tends to be much more common than was the case a few years ago.

It is current government policy to encourage the provision of pensions through the private sector and to reduce dependence on the state scheme. To this end, new legislation set out in the Social Security Act 1986 and the second Finance Act 1987 brought in a number of fundamental changes in the pension scene, which took effect from 1 July 1988, as follows.

1 The promotion of new *personal pension plans* for employees which would have the following features:

(a) the tax privileges already available in conventional pension schemes, in particular deductibility up to certain limits of employees' contributions;

(b) the ability for the individual to take his scheme with him when he changes jobs;

(c) the facility to contract out of SERPS if the individual wishes.

The operation of these plans is described in detail in question 45.

2 The simplification of arrangements whereby an individual already in an occupational pension scheme can 'top up' his pension fund so as to maximise his benefits. This is done by paying *additional voluntary contributions* (AVC's).

3 The introduction of *simplified occupational pension schemes* to encourage more employers to set up schemes.

4 The encouragement of *industry-wide occupational schemes*.

5 Improved *transferability* between different types of scheme.

One feature of this change will be the appearance of new 'pension providers', such as banks and building societies, as a result of the new financial services legislation.

The new pensions regime provides a much wider choice than was previously the case, particularly for employees. So much depends on an individual's career intentions and aspirations that it is difficult to provide, within the scope of this booklet, more than the most general advice; a number of more specialised publications on this subject are available and 'pension providers' are producing a variety of new pension products, accompanied by persuasive material as to why these are superior to everybody else's! Individuals should seek specialist and (if possible) objective advice, but meanwhile the following brief comments may be helpful:

1 If you have no company scheme and, for one reason or another, your employer is not going to implement one, then your only option is to start a personal pension policy for yourself. Depending on your age, it may be advantageous to use the plan to contract out of SERPS so as to gain an even better deal for yourself.

2 If you are in a company scheme there is likely to be little virtue in moving out of it and into a personal pension arrangement. However, if you are under 30 *and* are likely to change jobs, perhaps several times (this is becoming increasingly common in some occupations), you may well suffer some loss of benefit from continued membership of the company scheme and a personal pension plan may be better.

Remember, however, that if you do leave your company scheme, your employer is under no obligation to contribute anything at all to your personal scheme. You will need to weigh the advantages of continuity of your personal pension contributions against the benefits, perhaps interrupted or penalised if you leave, that will flow from your own and your employer's company scheme contributions.

3 The various factors that you need to take into account are these:
(a) your age;
(b) whether or not you are already in a scheme;
(c) what type of scheme you are in or may be eligible to join;
(d) how much you are or will be required to contribute to the scheme;
(e) how much your employer is contributing to the company scheme (and whether he will be willing to contribute anything to a personal scheme);
(f) how likely you are to change your job.

One important change that was introduced in the 1989 Budget set an upper limit of £60,000 a year on the amount of employment earnings for which contributions could be paid into an approved company scheme; this restriction applies to all new schemes set up after 13 March 1989 and to employees who join an existing scheme on or after 1 June 1989. The £60,000 limit is to be adjusted annually in line with the increase in the retail prices index; thus for 1990/91 it has been increased to £64,800.

If you are self-employed you may wish to prepare for your retirement by taking out a *retirement annuity policy* or, after 1 July 1988, a personal pension policy as described above (see question 45). There is a considerable range of self-employed pension schemes available, and the tax relief on the premiums must not be forgotten.

17 What national insurance contributions should I pay?

Broadly, the amount of contributions payable depends on whether the individual is employed, self-employed or non-employed. There are numerous variations for people in particular circumstances and the Department of Social Security publishes leaflets providing advice and guidance as to these. A brief summary of the general principles applicable to individuals in the three main categories mentioned is set out below. The contribution scales for 1989/90 and 1990/91 are given in Appendix 4.

Employees: Contributions are payable under Class 1 by both employees and employers on a sliding scale related to earnings. No contributions are payable where earnings are below £43 per week in 1989/90 or £46 per week in 1990/91. On earnings in excess of £350 per week in 1990/91 (£325 per week in 1989/90), no contributions are payable by employees although contributions continue to be payable by employers.

Where the employer has contracted out of the state scheme (see question 16), lower rates of contributions apply to earnings below £350 per week (£325 in 1989/90).

An employee does not have to pay Class 1 contributions after age 65 (60 for a woman) provided he gives his employer a certificate of age exemption.

Self-employed: Contributions are payable in two ways by all self-employed individuals; *Class 2* contributions at a flat rate and *Class 4* contributions at 6.3% on profits earned between certain limits. Half the amount of Class 4 contributions paid for a tax year are allowable as a deduction from the individual's total income for tax purposes for that year.

Where an individual is self-employed and also an employee, he is liable to pay Class 1 and 2 contributions (and possibly Class 4). Any excess will be refunded and it may be possible to arrange deferment of the Class 2 and 4 contributions until after the end of the year to avoid the need for a refund.

Non-employed: Voluntary flat rate contributions may be paid by an individual who wishes to improve his Class 1 or 2 contributions record to help in qualifying for a limited range of benefits.

● **18 If I am over 65 years of age, do I still pay tax?**

Unfortunately, the UK tax system is not run in such a way as to automatically exempt you from tax when you reach the age of 65. If you are able to continue working after the normal retirement age, you will continue to pay tax on your income, and if you are receiving a pension, this too is taxable.

There is, however, an allowance which will be granted if you are 65 or over in a year of assessment and your income falls within certain limits. In the case of a married couple it can be either the husband *or* the wife who is 65 or over to qualify for the relief.

This relief may be index-linked in the same way as the other main personal allowances. The reliefs and income limits for 1989/90 were as follows:

	Age	
	65–74	75 or over
Single person	£ 3,400	£ 3,540
Married man	£ 5,385	£ 5,565
Income limit	£11,400	£11,400

Note that the income limit is applied regardless of whether the taxpayer is single or married and in the case of a married couple applied to their joint income (following the general principle that the wife's income was assessable on the husband).

It should be noted that age allowance was *not* available where the election for the separate taxation of the wife's earnings (see question 8) was in operation. In practice this is not as hard as it sounds: if the individual's earnings were sufficient to justify making the election, it is most unlikely that age allowance would have been applicable in any case.

A word of warning here. Where the individual's total income exceeded the income limit shown above by a small amount the allowance was reduced by £1 for every £2 of excess income, until the amount came down to the level of the normal single person's or married man's allowance. This could have a marked effect on the rate of tax applicable to the excess income, as the following example illustrates.

Example

Mr Senior, a married man aged 70, had a total income of £10,800 in the tax year 1989/90. His tax liability on this would have been:

	£
Total income	10,800
Age allowance	5,385
Chargeable to tax	£5,415
Income tax at 25%	£1,354

Now, if his income for 1989/90 was £11,800, the calculation becomes:

		£
Total income		11,800
Age allowance	5,385	
Less Abatement half of		
(11,800−11,400)	200	5,185
Chargeable to tax		£6,615
Income tax at 25%		£1,654

Mr Senior would therefore have had to pay extra tax of £300 on the additional income of £1,000, an effective rate of 30%!

With the introduction of independent taxation of married couples (see question 9), the system is preserved but with some modifications. The reliefs and income limit, for 1990/91 are as follows:

	Age	
	65–74	75 or over
Single personal age allowance	£ 3,670	£ 3,820
Married couple's age allowance	£ 2,145	£ 2,185
Income limit	£12,300	£12,300

To illustrate the operation of these allowances in figures (assuming no income restrictions):

Husband aged 67	(3,670 + 2,145)	£5,815
Wife aged 66		£3,670
Husband aged 64	(3,005 + 2,145)	£5,150
Wife aged 66		£3,670

In the second example quoted above, it will be seen that the husband suffers some disadvantage in the changeover to independent taxation; in 1989/90 he was entitled to the higher age allowance for a married man because *his wife* was over 65, but in 1990/91 he only receives the normal single personal allowance because *he* is under that age. To overcome this anomaly, for 1990/91 the husband will receive the age allowance of £3,670 instead of the normal allowance of £3,005. In the example given, in 1991/92 the husband will be 65 and will therefore qualify for age allowance; if he were then still under 65, the transitional relief would continue to be available but only at the 1990/91 level. He does of course in any event receive the married couple's age allowance of £2,145. A similar arrangement applies where the husband is under 75 but the wife was over 75 in 1989/90.

For a married couple the income limit and the marginal restriction described above now applies to each spouse separately. This does considerably widen the scope of the relief as compared with previous years as the following example will demonstrate.

Example

Mr and Mrs Elder are both aged 68. He has a pension from his company of £9,000 and a state retirement pension of £2,140. She also receives a state pension based on his contributions of £1,287 and investment income of £8,250.

Under the previous law, Mr and Mrs Elder's combined incomes of £20,677 would have ruled out any claim to age allowance and they would have been entitled only to the normal personal allowances. Under the new law each is under the income limit of £11,400 and therefore qualifies for age allowance without restriction, as follows:

		£
Mr Elder		
Company pension		9,000
State pension		2,140
		11,140
Less age allowances		
single personal	3,670	
married couple's	2,145	5,815
Chargeable to tax		£5,325
Income tax at 25%		£1,331

Mrs Elder

State pension	1,287
Investment income	8,250
	9,537
Less age allowance	3,670
Chargeable to tax	£5,867
Income tax at 25%	£1,467

Where the income limit does come into play, the individual may like to consider putting money into investments which will produce capital gains rather than income. Commonly, as explained in Chapter 5, such gains would be covered by the annual exemption (£5,000 in 1990/91) and the indexation allowance.

Other possible arrangements that can be used are:
1 Investing in National Savings Certificates (see question 23) and cashing these in at regular intervals to take advantage of the tax-free interest additions;
2 Investing in an investment bond (see question 23) and making annual withdrawals from this. Providing that these do not exceed 5% of the original cost per year, they will not normally be subject to income tax.

19 Are all social security benefits taxable?

There are approximately 40 different benefits which are payable by the Department of Social Security which are *not taxable*; these include maternity benefit and grants, invalidity pensions, student grants, family income supplement, child benefit, sickness benefit and mobility allowance.

The benefits listed below are all taxable as earned income:
Industrial death benefit
Invalid care allowance
Invalidity allowance when paid with retirement pension
Old person's pension
Retirement pension
War orphan's pension
Widowed mother's allowance
Widow's allowance

Widow's pension
Unemployment benefit
Certain privately-operated sickness scheme benefits.

20   What income tax reliefs can I claim in respect of my home?

If you do not own your own home you cannot claim any allowance
for the rent you pay. If you are buying your own home for which you
have taken out a mortgage with a building society or other lender,
you may wish to claim tax relief on the interest paid each year, thus
reducing the amount of your taxable income.

Loans for the purchase of land, including buildings, are specifically allowable for tax purposes, provided certain conditions are
met. Loans for the improvement of a property may also qualify for
relief but only where taken out on or before 5 April 1988.

At the time the interest is paid the property must be the sole or
main residence of the borrower or of a separated spouse. The loan
must be used for the purposes of purchasing or improving the house,
and not just by way of borrowing capital using the house as security.
The relief is limited to the first £30,000 of the loan. For loans taken
out on or after 1 August 1988, a further restriction applies to limit
the amount qualifying for interest relief to £30,000 *per property*,
irrespective of the number of borrowers involved. Where there is
more than one borrower the interest relief is divided between them
in the same ratio as the borrowing. Also allowable for income tax
purposes is a bridging loan taken out for the purchase of one
residence with a view to a previous residence being sold; again the
relief is limited to the first £30,000 of the loan.

Where husband and wife are joint borrowers the interest relief is
normally allocated equally between them; each will be subject to a
£15,000 loan limit. However they can elect to divide the interest
between them in any other proportion that suits them on giving an
appropriate joint election to the Revenue. The election must be
made within 12 months of the end of the tax year for which it is to
apply and will continue to operate for subsequent years until it is
varied or withdrawn, within the same 12 months time limit; it may
not be withdrawn for the first year that it is in force but it may be
varied by submitting a new election.

It should be emphasised that in any case tax relief can only be
claimed on the interest element of mortgage payments and not on
capital repayments.

This relief was also available for a loan taken out up to 5 April 1988 for the purchase or improvement of a property used as the sole or main residence of a dependent relative of the borrower (or his/her spouse) who lived there rent-free. (See question 70 for capital gains tax implications of this situation.)

The next question you will no doubt ask is actually how to claim the tax relief due on the interest payments. Until 6 April 1983, payments were made gross and tax relief was given in PAYE coding or by assessment. After that date, for most people, payments are made under the MIRAS scheme. This stands for 'mortgage interest relief at source' and enables the payer to obtain the benefit of tax relief at the basic rate by deducting it from the gross amount and paying only the net amount to the lender.

If you are a basic rate taxpayer, once the net payment has been made there is no further tax relief due. However, if you are liable to pay tax at a higher rate you are entitled to further relief which will normally be given in your PAYE coding or in the assessment.

You cannot normally claim for the day-to-day running of your home but if you use part of your home as an office you may be able to claim a tax allowance in respect of lighting and heating, etc. The Revenue is sometimes reluctant to allow such claims, taking the view that if an employer requires you to do 'paperwork' he will provide you with an office. However, claims are accepted if you prove it is *necessary* to work at home, whether you are an employee or self-employed. *Beware*, however, of making a claim that you use part of your home *exclusively* for these purposes as you may find the exemption from capital gains tax (CGT) on your own home is affected (see question 69).

21 What other loan interest can I claim?

The rules regarding relief for other loan interest are very strict and relief will not be granted unless the loan proceeds applied for meet the qualifying purpose within a reasonable length of time. Similarly, if the loan is used for some other purpose first, the relief will not be granted. There is no tax relief for overdraft interest or credit cards (or similar arrangements), unless it is incurred wholly and exclusively for the purposes of your business as a sole trader or partner and is charged directly in your business accounts.

Loan interest relief will be allowed if the proceeds of the loan are used for any of the following, all of which are *qualifying purposes:*

1 A loan in respect of property which is let at a commercial rent for at least 26 weeks of the year and when not being let is available to be let or is undergoing repair. There may be some restrictions as to the relief available, but these do not apply when the property qualifies as furnished holiday accommodation (see question 26).

2 Provision is also made to cover the situation where the borrower is living in accommodation provided by the employer as one of the requirements of his job (referred to as *job-related accommodation*), but at the same time the employee is paying interest on a loan to buy a house which he is either using as a residence at the time or intends to so use within 12 months; this allows relief to be claimed for interest paid by the employee on a loan on a house bought in anticipation of moving out of his present accommodation. A similar relief is available where the individual is self-employed and is required to live in 'job-related' accommodation. Relief is in any case limited to interest on a maximum £30,000 loan.

3 A loan for purchase of plant or machinery for use in a trade if the borrower is a partner in the business, or for use in the borrower's office or employment. Relief is only granted in the tax year in which the loan is taken out and the following three years, and only if a claim for capital allowances on the plant and machinery has been granted.

4 A loan for the purchase of ordinary shares in, or making a loan to, a close company, subject to certain restrictions.

5 A loan for purchase of a share in, or making a loan to, a partnership. The lender must be a member of the partnership; where the money is lent to the partnership it must be used for the purposes of the partnership business.

6 A loan to make payment of capital transfer tax, estate duty or inheritance tax in respect of a deceased person. The relief is granted to the personal representatives, but for a period of one year only from the date of the loan.

7 A loan (up to a maximum of £30,000) to purchase a life annuity by a borrower aged 65 or over. He must use his own home as security for the loan and at least 90% of the proceeds of the loan must be used to purchase the annuity (see question 23).

8 A loan to buy shares in an 'employee-controlled company'; this can arise where employees are given the opportunity to buy a controlling interest in an unquoted company from its existing proprietors (this again may be subject to some restrictions, depending mainly on the percentage shareholding acquired by the individual).

● 22   Do I pay tax on my building society or bank interest?

As with most forms of investment income, interest on deposit, savings, investment and similar accounts with *banks* and *building societies* is paid after deduction of tax. At present a special rate known as the *composite rate*, which is slightly less than the basic rate of income tax, is used; this is intended to reflect the average rate of tax borne by such investors, recognising that some of them do not pay tax at all. As a corollary to this, a recipient who is not liable to income tax is *not* able to claim any refund of this tax withheld by the bank or building society. On the other hand, a recipient who is liable to income tax is treated as having received the interest as if tax *at the basic rate* had been deducted: if he is only liable to tax at the basic rate, no further tax is payable; if he is liable to tax at higher rates, the additional tax will be assessed on him directly.

Up to 5 April 1985 *bank* interest was *not* taxed before receipt and it was therefore wholly taxable in the recipient's hands. The normal basis of assessment was on the 'preceding year', i.e. whatever was credited to your bank account in one tax year was taxed in the following tax year. There were special rules for the interest credited during the opening and closing years of a bank account when the interest could be taxed in the same year that it was credited to the account.

It should be noted, however, that certain types of bank deposit accounts do allow the interest to be paid without tax being deducted. This may apply for example to time deposits in excess of £50,000. Also composite rate tax does *not* apply to a bank deposit account held outside the UK, for instance at the Jersey branch of a UK bank, by an individual who is resident in this country. Interest on such an account will continue to be paid gross and assessed to income tax on the recipient as described above.

An individual who is *not ordinarily resident* in this country (see question 34) with a deposit account at a UK branch may apply to his bank or building society to have the interest credited to him gross.

Bodies such as charities which are exempt from tax may also arrange to have bank and building society interest paid to them gross.

Interest on certain deposits with *local authorities* continued to be paid gross until 5 April 1986, after which the composite rate tax system applied to them also.

With effect from *6 April 1991*, this system will be abolished. Thereafter banks, building societies and local authorities will pay interest after deduction of tax at the normal basic rate; the position of taxpayers who are already liable to tax at the basic or higher rates will not be affected (except that the net amount paid to them may be marginally reduced), but those individuals who are not liable to income tax at all will be able to reclaim the amount deducted. Furthermore, a self-certification procedure will be available to non-taxpayers whereby they will be able to certify to the bank, etc. that they are not liable to tax on the interest and have it paid to them gross.

Interest credited to the National Savings Bank *ordinary* account is exempt up to £70 a year for an individual. If you are married, each spouse will be entitled to the £70 exemption but any excess of one spouse's exemption *cannot* be given to the other. Any interest in excess of £70 is still paid gross but liable to tax in the usual way. This exemption *does not* apply to the National Savings Bank *investment* account, where the interest is paid gross and taxable on the recipient in full.

23 Where should I invest my capital?

This is a topic which could be the subject matter of a book in its own right. There is no answer because matters such as the availability of your capital (i.e. the need to have quick access to capital), provision for your dependents, how much you want to invest and your own personal tax position must be taken into consideration. It is therefore not possible to list different forms of investment and to advise on which ones to use without knowing about your overall financial position – this is something for you to discuss with your professional advisers. What follows, therefore, are a few *general* words of advice.

There are certain types of investments on which you *do not* pay tax; these include the *National Savings Bank* ordinary account (see question 22) where up to £70 interest can be credited to your account without tax being payable. There are also *National Savings Certificates*, on which interest, bonuses and any other sums are exempt from all forms of tax; there is a limit to the number of these you may hold. These include a special index-linked issue. You may wish to invest in *Premium Bonds* – if you do so, remember there is no interest on the amount invested but if you should win a prize, your winnings are not taxable.

You may also invest in the *National Savings Yearly Plan*. This allows you to subscribe a regular amount from £20 to £200 per month to buy a *Yearly Plan Savings Certificate* at the end of the year. These certificates earn a guaranteed rate of interest (tax free) which increases the longer the certificates are held.

Many people invest their capital in *building societies* and the interest they receive is net of tax. A point to note arises here: if you are not liable to pay tax at all, investing your money in a building society or in a bank deposit account in the UK is *not* a good idea, as you are deemed to have paid tax on the interest but this cannot be reclaimed, as explained in question 22.

The rate of interest on ordinary share accounts is quite reasonable but if you do not require immediate access to your capital a *Save As You Earn (SAYE) Scheme* through a building society, a bank or National Savings may provide a better return. Such an investment is one of the best ways to earn a high rate of interest, but it is a longer term commitment to saving, as you will be required to pay a fixed sum every month for a period of up to five years. Beware of stopping the payments early as penalties can be incurred.

Whatever the amount of capital you wish to invest you will obviously require a certain amount that is realisable to provide cash in an emergency; you may wish to consider investing in *government gilt-edged stocks*. The income you receive from these investments is taxed at source (at the basic rate of tax) and there is now no liability to capital gains tax (see question 68).

Certain issues of gilt-edged stocks are inflation linked, providing a measure of tax-free capital appreciation which would be attractive to higher rate tax payers.

Another form of long-term investment is the *single premium investment bond*. A capital sum is invested with an insurance company; the income is taxable but you are allowed to withdraw each year up to 5% of the initial value invested and these withdrawals are not immediately taxed. They are taken into account in the year the bond is surrendered, so that higher rate tax may be payable in this final year. It is possible, however, to reduce this liability with careful planning, by making sure that the year of encashment is one when other income and therefore tax rates are low. It should be appreciated that the insurance company will already have borne tax at 35% on the amounts added to the value of the bond.

If you are already a higher-rate taxpayer you should be seeking to minimise your tax liability, possibly by aiming for capital growth. Although capital gains are now taxed at income tax rates, some advantage may be obtained through the CGT indexation allowance and annual exemption (see question 65). This may result in you having to withdraw from time to time capital to supplement your income, unless you also have other forms of investment.

If you are considering investing directly on the stock market, for many people unit trusts represent the most sensible and effective way of doing so. The clearing banks and TSB offer a wide range of savings schemes which could also be considered.

In 1987 another form of tax efficient investment, known as the *personal equity plan* (PEP), was introduced as an incentive to encourage savings through the purchase of quoted shares. This allows an individual to invest up to £6,000 a year (which may be in regular monthly amounts or in a lump sum) through an authorised plan manager, such as a bank or stockbroker, in a separate fund on his behalf. Provided that a number of conditions are satisfied, interest and dividends on the plan investments that are reinvested in the plan are free of income tax. A similar exemption from CGT applies to reinvested capital gains.

It should be noted that the plan manager will levy certain charges for his services, which will reduce the value of the income tax exemption. So far as the CGT exemption is concerned, an investor is entitled to an annual exemption in any case (£5,000 in 1990/91, see question 65). Thus the PEP's exemption may not be of any value unless the investor expects to use up his annual exemption elsewhere.

A development of the PEP announced in the 1990 Budget is the *tax exempt special savings account* (TESSA). With effect from 1 January 1991 any individual over the age of 18 will be able to open one (but not more than one) of these accounts with a bank or building society and subject to the conditions which follow the interest earned on the account will be entirely tax free.

The account will have to run for five years. Up to £9,000 may be deposited in the account over this five year period; not more than £1,800 may be invested in any one year except that up to £3,000 may be deposited in the first year. Within these limits a TESSA will be very flexible so that it could appeal to someone who wants to save on a regular basis, to someone who already has savings and wants to supplement his income by generating interest tax free or to someone who can only save irregularly.

45

No part of the capital may be withdrawn during the five year period and only interest net of basic rate tax; both capital and the tax withheld may be freely withdrawn after the five years. Any breach of these conditions will result in the tax exemption being totally withdrawn.

An investment that may be of interest to the elderly is a *purchased life annuity*. This is where an individual invests some of his capital in an annuity; when he receives the annuity payments at a later date, part of the payment is treated as the return of his capital and is not taxed; the remainder is taxed as unearned income. The split between capital and income will depend on the individual's age at the date of commencement of the annuity. There is *no tax relief on the cost of buying the annuity*.

It is also possible for an individual aged over 65 to borrow (up to a maximum of £30,000) on the security of his house and provided that at least 90% of the loan is used to buy an annuity for himself (or him and his wife jointly) he can obtain tax relief on the loan interest paid (see question 21).

With an uncertain future with regard to inflation, it is wise to have a *flexible investment policy* rather than allow yourself to become too restricted. It might well be prudent, therefore, even if your aim is for a higher income, to invest some of your funds in investments producing lower income than perhaps could be obtained otherwise, in order to achieve *flexibility*, *security* for your capital and the prospects of *capital growth*.

● 24 Can I give money to charity in a tax efficient way?

The most obvious way in which you can provide financial aid to the charity of your choice with the support of the Inland Revenue is through the use of a *deed of covenant*.

This is defined as the 'gratuitous transfer' by one person (the donor) of some part of his income for a defined period to another person (the charity). Provided that the period set down in the deed (i.e. the agreement between the donor and the charity) is capable of exceeding three years (hence most such deeds require a commitment for at least four years), the donor is treated as making the payment out of his net income after tax, i.e. so that it represents income from which income tax at the basic rate has already been deducted. This has two consequences as follows.

1 The recipient charity is able to treat such receipts as income

which has already suffered tax. As every recognised charity is exempt from tax on income of this kind it is able to recover the income tax treated as deducted from the payment made by the donor.

2 The donor is able to claim relief for higher rate tax purposes for the payments made in this way.

Consider the following example, using 1990/91 tax rates.

Example:

Mr Scrooge covenants to pay the Tiny Tim Charity an annual amount after deduction of tax of £75 for four years.

		£
Tiny Tim Charity:		
Amount received per year		75
Income tax treated as deducted, recoverable by charity		25
Gross income to charity		£100
Mr Scrooge:		
Gross equivalent of payments, as above		100
Income tax relief to donor		
basic rate withheld at 25%	25	
higher rate at (40−25)%	15	40
Net cost to Mr Scrooge		£ 60

With the introduction of independent taxation for married couples from 6 April 1990 (see question 9), care has to be taken to ensure that where the wife enters into a charitable deed of covenant, she has sufficient taxed income to cover the covenanted payments; otherwise the arrangement is ineffective for tax purposes. In the example given above, if the covenant had been made by Mrs Scrooge instead of her husband and in 1990/91 it transpires that she did not have any income subject to tax, the Revenue could require her to pay over to them the income tax of £25 which she had been treated as deducting from the payment made to the charity. The charity would not be disadvantaged in these circumstances, but Mrs Scrooge certainly would be!

The Inland Revenue have recently issued guidance notes on the preparation of deeds of covenant to ensure that they are properly drawn up and executed.

Employers are able, if they wish, to operate a *payroll deduction scheme*, which enables them to arrange for their employees to authorise deductions from their pay to be paid over to specified charities. These deductions qualify for tax relief up to £600 a year.

A new form of charitable giving, known as *gift aid*, will be available from 1 October 1990. This will enable an individual to obtain income tax relief on single gifts of £600 or more in cash up to a maximum of £5 million in a year. The relief will operate in the same way as for deeds of covenant already described. The donor will deduct tax at the basic rate from the gift and will be able to obtain higher rate tax relief on it; the donee charity will be able to reclaim the tax from the Revenue.

● **25   Can I set aside money towards my taxes?**

It is possible to set money aside to pay your taxes by way of *certificates of tax deposit*. Some people prefer this method of payment of tax to having to withdraw money from another source to pay their tax bills. The deposits are made with the Collector of Taxes for the subsequent payment of tax generally (except for PAYE and tax deducted from subcontractors in the construction industry). The minimum initial deposit is £2,000 with minimum additions of £500. Interest is payable gross, but is taxable, and this will accrue for a maximum of six years from the date of deposit to the date the tax is due to be paid. If a deposit is withdrawn for cash at any time, a reduced rate of interest will apply.

● **26   I have other sources of income which are not taxed at source: how are they taxed?**

The most common of the other types of income you may receive which are not taxed at source are as follows.

Furnished lettings: An assessment is made on the profits arising in the year, which is rent received less rent paid, repairs, rates, commission and any other expenses relating to the letting. There are also allowances that may be claimed for wear and tear of the furniture.

The profit from lettings of *furnished holiday accommodation* may be treated as earned income provided that certain tests are met. The most important of these are:

(a) The property is available for letting to the general public as furnished residential accommodation for at least 140 days in the tax year.

(b) It is actually so let for at least 70 days.

(c) During a period of at least seven months (which need not be continuous but which does include the actual periods of letting in (b)), each occupancy does not normally exceed 31 days.

Income from other property: Tax is charged on rents received from property including rents from leases of land and buildings, ground rents, feu duties, etc. The assessments are made on the basis of receipts arising in the year of assessment, less allowable deductions such as repairs, rates, electricity, etc., insurance premiums, valuation fees, costs of rent collection.

Income arising overseas: The UK tax system is such that it taxes income wherever it arises if the person entitled to receive it is resident here. If you are entitled to receive income from overseas, due to the fact that other countries have similar wide powers of taxation, it is inevitable that some income will be taxed twice. Although it may be impossible to avoid this altogether, in many cases where income suffers tax in two countries it is possible to claim *double taxation relief*.

There are double taxation treaties between the UK and some 90 other countries and in general, either a particular source of income is exempt from tax in one of the countries involved, or the relief for foreign taxation is given as a credit against the corresponding UK tax.

This is a complex area and special consideration needs to be given to each situation.

2 YOU HAVE EARNED IT

TAXATION OF THE EMPLOYEE

● **27   What is included in my earnings for income tax purposes and how are they taxed under the PAYE system?**

Earnings from an office or employment come under many different names such as salaries, wages, fees, overtime, bonuses, commission, tips and gratuities, etc. *In general, anything which you receive as a reward for your services is taxable*, and the words 'emoluments' and 'remuneration' are often used to cover all receipts of this nature.

Having decided what is taxable, the next problem is how is it taxed? As an employee, you are probably only too well aware of the tax that is deducted from the pay you receive each week or month under the *Pay As You Earn* (PAYE) scheme.

The PAYE system was introduced in 1943 to replace other less successful methods of taxing the earnings of employees. It was not introduced as a new method of assessment; it was, and still is, merely a *scheme for the collection of tax*. Its aim is to deduct tax from each payment of remuneration, the deduction rising and falling as the pay rises and falls, so that at the end of the income tax year, the tax deducted during the year is sufficient having regard to the employee's personal circumstances and no further action is necessary.

The backbone of the system is the *cumulative* principle under which, as the tax year progresses, running (cumulative) totals are kept of the amounts of remuneration received from the beginning of the tax year and of the tax deducted. Each time your employer pays remuneration he will deduct (or refund) an amount of tax which will keep the total figure deducted correct. He can tell what this figure should be from tax tables which are supplied by the Inland Revenue. The process continues up to week 52 or month 12, when a new income tax year starts, and you commence at week 1 or month 1 again. Special procedures apply where there are 53 pay days in the year.

You already know that the amount of tax payable is governed by your personal circumstances and there are certain reliefs and allowances you may claim. If the employer is to deduct the right amount of tax it would seem that he too must have knowledge of your personal circumstances but the Revenue are bound not to reveal to anyone the private information given to them. The difficulty is resolved by the use of *codings*, with a number and a letter from which the employer can only tell certain things (i.e. in most cases he can tell if you are a single or married man, but if you do not wish him to know this, it can be prevented). The allowances to which you are entitled are added together and the coding applicable to this is notified to the employer – *the higher the coding, the lower the tax.* Your employer will only be informed of the final coding but you will be sent a notice showing your allowances and how the resulting coding is arrived at; if you disagree with it you may appeal against it, following the procedure described in question 3. Similarly, if your personal circumstances change during the year the Revenue should be notified and your coding will be amended. Because of the cumulative principle mentioned above, a change of coding has retrospective effect to the previous 6 April. If it is increased, the tax overdeducted in previous weeks or months is refunded by your employer. If it is decreased, a special basis called week 1 or month 1 is used as otherwise the tax underdeducted in the previous weeks would be deductible in one sum, and this could cause hardship. In effect, in this situation the cumulative principle is abandoned for that year, and the employer deducts tax on each pay day without reference to previous pay. (See question 28 for what happens to the tax underdeducted for the earlier part of the year.)

The previous paragraphs may give the impression that employees stay with one employer all the time but, of course, people change their jobs, school leavers start work for the first time, people retire and in fact there is a constant movement. To cater for this within the PAYE system, when you leave one employer he will give you a form known as a P45 which shows your coding, pay and tax to date. This form must be given to your new employer to enable him to continue the cumulative deductions of tax. If you lose your P45, or for some other reason are starting work without one, your employer will use a special coding so that your tax does not fall too far into arrears, and will inform the Revenue so that they may start the procedure for issuing the correct coding.

It should be noted that unemployment benefit is taxable as earned income (see question 19). The actual benefit payments are made without deduction of tax to benefit claimants, but these are then taken into account in determining whether any part of the tax deducted under PAYE prior to the period of unemployment is to be refunded. Any refund is made only when the individual starts work again or at the end of the tax year, whichever is the sooner.

● **28   If I pay tax under PAYE will I also be assessed at the end of each year? If so, how will I be assessed?**

It has already been explained that the PAYE system is not a method of assessment but simply a way of collecting the tax. The next point to consider is how much of the earnings are assessed for a particular year. *The proper basis of assessment is to assess the amount actually earned in the year of assessment.* Most employees receive at the end of each week or month the amount of money they have actually earned during that period. If at the end of the tax year they are therefore assessed on what they have earned, this is the same figure as the amount they have received and tax has already been deducted. The employer sends to the Revenue details of each person's pay and tax deducted on what is called a *deduction working sheet* – the details are checked and if the tax deducted is correct, no further action is normally required.

If you ask for an assessment because you think you have paid the wrong amount of tax the Revenue will do as you ask, but the Revenue also has the right to make an assessment where they consider it is appropriate, for example where they realise that, for whatever reason, too little tax has been deducted in the year. This includes situations where there is tax owing for an earlier year or where an allowance has been given incorrectly. Any refund of tax due to you resulting from the assessment is repaid to you, but if there is an underpayment of tax this will be collected from you.

This is normally achieved by restricting your coding allowances for the following year, although there are occasions when you will be asked to make payment of the tax to the Collector of Taxes; this usually applies where the underpayment exceeds £350. Also collected through a later coding adjustment are underpayments arising because an allowance was removed from the coding part way through a year and there is tax to pay for the period before the coding was amended. If, in any of these instances, to collect the tax in one year would cause hardship this may be spread over a period of up to three years. No action is taken to collect small amounts (up to £30) and a lenient view is taken of pensioners.

29 How much can I receive tax free if I cease my employment?

First of all, one very important point must be made – if you have a contract of employment which provides for a termination payment, that sum is taxable in full. Apart from this, termination payments may be made (on or after 6 April 1988) tax free up to £30,000; amounts in excess are taxable as income in the usual way. (Note that it is the date of *termination* that is critical for these purposes, *not* the date of payment.)

For payments related to terminations taking place prior to 6 April 1988, the reliefs operated as follows:
– on the first £25,000, tax free;
– on the next £25,000, the tax payable is reduced by a half;
– on the next £25,000 the tax payable is reduced by a quarter;
– on the excess over £75,000, tax is payable in full.

A payment in lieu of notice cannot be taxed at the time that it is made, as it is not regarded as remuneration (even if it is made under a clause in the contract of employment, because this option is in any case open to an employer under the employment legislation). However, it must be included with any other termination payments for the purpose of applying the reliefs mentioned in the previous paragraph.

It is important that termination payments are correctly identified and that references to them in correspondence, minutes of board meetings, etc. are worded in a way that does not suggest that they are payments for past or future services as then they could be charged to tax as income from that employment.

To obtain the maximum benefit for this relief it is helpful to keep other income as low as possible in the year in which the payment is taxable; thus, if a new employment is to be taken up immediately, termination should be as near to the end of the tax year as possible.

Statutory redundancy payments as such are exempt from tax but will still need to be taken into account in these calculations.

A rather curious situation came to light in June 1986. The law relating to termination payments was amended in 1982, as set out at the beginning of this question. But owing to a drafting error that slice of the termination payment on which tax was to be reduced by a half was fixed at £50,000, not £25,000 as intended and indeed as everybody (Inland Revenue, professional advisers and tax-payers) believed. When this error was discovered, the law was hurriedly corrected with effect from 4 June 1986 so as to ensure that only £25,000 ranked for relief in this way.

However, the correction was not made retrospective, so that it is possible if an individual was entitled to a termination payment of more than £50,000 in the period 6 April 1982 to 3 June 1986, both dates inclusive, he may now be entitled to make a supplementary claim for relief and to receive a repayment of tax. This could amount to as much as £7,500 (i.e. half of £25,000 at 60%) plus repayment supplement (see question 5). Any such supplementary claim must be made within six years of the end of the tax year in which the termination of employment took place.

30 Are perks taxable?

Most employees like a job that has perks and many employers nowadays run some form of incentive scheme or give their employees a benefit of some description. Unfortunately, the majority of these *fringe benefits*, as they are called, are taxable, although in some cases this depends on whether you are an employee (commonly referred to as a *higher paid employee*) whose earnings are at a rate of £8,500 a year or more or a director (in which case the level of your remuneration is irrelevant). It should be noted that 'remuneration' is specially defined for the purpose of this £8,500 threshold, so as to include the value of benefits and of expenses reimbursed before any deductions are allowed. Because of the method of taxing fringe benefits, it is nearly always to your advantage to be given an item as a benefit instead of having to pay for the same item out of your own net income which has already suffered tax.

It is not possible to list in this book all the possible benefits your employer may consider but the following table mentions some of the more popular choices.

The special rules relating to company cars (still far and away the most popular perk) are dealt with in question 31.

As has already been stated, this is only a brief outline of the taxation of some of the fringe benefits: if you wish to know more about these matters you should seek professional advice.

Benefit	Employees earning over £8,500 per annum and directors	Employees earning less than £8,500 per annum
Holidays	Taxable in full unless combined with a business trip when the 'holiday element' may still be taxable	Not taxable providing employer pays direct and does not reimburse employee
Season tickets	Taxable	Taxable
Suggestion scheme payments	Not taxable provided it is within specified limits and not a term of contract	Same as directors
Prize incentive schemes	Taxable	Taxable
Examination prizes	Taxable	Taxable
Canteen facilities	Not taxable provided available in one form or another to *all* staff	Not taxable
Luncheon vouchers	Not taxable provided not in excess of 15p per day. Excess over 15p taxable	Same as directors
Seminars/external courses/ conferences	Not generally taxable if borne and paid for by the employer	Not taxable
Credit cards	Taxable	Taxable
Community charge ('poll tax')	Taxable	Taxable

Benefit	Employees earning over £8,500 per annum and directors	Employees earning less than £8,500 per annum
Medical insurance	Taxable on cost to employer. If taken out for groups of employees, each is taxable on proportion of cost. *Not* taxable if insurance against cost of treatment abroad where occasioned while employee performing duties outside UK	Not taxable
Welfare, sports and social facilities	Not taxable	Not taxable
Use of company-owned assets by employees, e.g. furniture, housing, cars	Taxable on 'annual value' when use begins; generally 20% of cost of asset, special rules for houses, cars	Not taxable
Transfer of company-owned assets other than cars to employees	Taxable on market value when first used by employee less benefit already charged to him (as above) or on market value at time of transfer, if greater	Taxable on market value at time of transfer
Transfer of company car to employee	Taxable on market value at time of transfer	Same as directors
Scholarships awarded to employees' children	Taxable	Not taxable

Benefit	Employees earning over £8,500 per annum and directors	Employees earning less than £8,500 per annum
Workplace nurseries	Up to 5 April 1985 by *concession* not taxable. Taxable from 6 April 1985. Not taxable by *law* from 6 April 1990	Not taxable
Car parking	Not taxable from 6 April 1988	Same as directors

31 What is my tax position if I have a company car or use my own car for business purposes?

If you are provided with a company car and you use it for your own private purposes, you are obviously deriving a benefit from this, simply due to the fact that you are using a car that does not belong to you for your own private use. On the other hand, if you are using your own car for business purposes this must benefit your employer and if he does not reimburse the expenses you incur, you would be out of pocket.

If you are a director or a higher paid employee (as defined, see question 30) and you have a company car, you are taxed on what the Revenue considers is the benefit you receive from using the car for your own use. This is often referred to as the 'table benefit' because the benefit is decided according to the age, cost and cylinder capacity of the car, set out in tables included in the legislation. If your business mileage exceeds 18,000 the benefit is *reduced to one half*. On the other hand, if your business mileage is less than 2,500 miles a year the benefit is increased to one and a half times the normal figure; this increase also applies to a second car provided by the employer. If you use your own car for business purposes you may claim a tax allowance as if you are self-employed (see question 39) but when the allowance has been computed any amount received from your employer by way of reimbursement is deducted.

Petrol provided by an employer for the private use of a director or higher paid employee is also taxed according to tables similar to those referred to in the previous paragraph. See also question 99 regarding the VAT treatment of petrol provided for private use with effect from 6 April 1987 onwards.

The tables of the car and car petrol benefits for 1989/90 and 1990/91 are shown in Appendix 3.

Where the employee is required to make a contribution to the employer for the private use of the car, the corresponding 'car' benefit is reduced by that amount. However, no reduction is made to the 'car petrol' benefit for any contribution towards the cost of petrol unless the employee is required to reimburse that amount provided for private use *and* does so, *or* if petrol is made available only for business use; in that case, the car petrol benefit is reduced to nil. No reduction is made where the employee is required to reimburse a proportion of the petrol cost or if he makes a voluntary contribution towards the cost. It follows that where an employee does make some contribution towards his employer's costs, this should, as far as possible, be attributed to the use of the car, thus reducing the taxable benefit, rather than to the provision of petrol, with no such reduction.

Where an employee has a relatively low private mileage, it may be to his advantage to forego the car petrol benefit altogether and pay for his own private petrol.

In any event *no allowance* is given for *travelling between home and work* as this is not classed as business mileage. The rule is that such expenses must be incurred *wholly and exclusively* in 'the performance of the duties of the employment' to be allowable and this does not generally cover travelling expenses *to or from* that place of employment (see question 32).

32 Are there any other expenses I can claim?

It cannot be emphasised too often that expenses are only allowable if they are incurred *wholly, exclusively and necessarily in the performance of the duties* of your employment. There must therefore be no question of the expenses being partly for your own benefit and they must be absolutely necessary for you to carry out your duties. Many of the claims made to the Revenue which fail, do so on the test of necessity.

You have already seen that the costs of travelling between home and work are generally not deductible because the costs are not incurred in the course of performing the duties but in order to get to the place where the duties are to be performed. Travelling expenses *will* be allowed provided they are incurred wholly and exclusively in the performance of the duties of the office. However, as mentioned in question 31 in connection with car mileage, 'travelling' does not normally include travel between home and the place of employment. This is based on the principle that the duties of the employment are performed at the place of employment and not on the way there or back. Thus the reimbursement of such expenses will generally be taxable on the employee. This rule may be modified where the employee is required to use his home as his base and only occasionally visits his office (e.g. a sales representative) or where exceptional late night travel is involved. It is generally accepted that travel expenses include the cost of accommodation while travelling.

You may wish to make a claim that part of your home is used as an office – this is covered in question 20. If, in addition to this, you purchase books, etc., you may find it difficult to prove that they are wholly, exclusively and necessarily for the performance of your duties. If you pay subscriptions to a *recognised* body, such as a professional institute, the amount you pay is, by a specific provision in the law, allowable as an expense.

Similarly, if you are a manual worker there are often fixed deductions agreed, depending on the actual nature of your employment and the industry in which you are employed.

33 How can I check that my PAYE coding is correct?

As mentioned in question 27, a notice should be sent to each employee showing what allowances he is entitled to (or considered by the Revenue to be entitled to) and how his PAYE coding is arrived at. In practice, a notice of coding is not necessarily issued each year and it may therefore be helpful if an employee carries out his own check against the Revenue's coding as operated by his employer. The employee will need to follow this procedure.
1 Add up the allowances: for most people this will be the single person's allowance plus, if applicable, the married couple's allowance (see questions 7 and 9);
2 Deduct from 1 the amounts of any benefits in kind taxable on him (see question 30 and 31);
3 Also deduct any restriction for underpaid PAYE for earlier years (see question 28);
4 Divide the result by ten.

This result, ignoring the last digit, should be the individual's coding.

A typical example of this for 1990/91 might be as shown in the following table.

Note that no adjustment is made for mortgage interest paid under MIRAS (see question 20), unless the individual is a higher rate taxpayer, nor is there an adjustment for any life assurance premiums paid (see question 12), as the relief due will normally be given by deduction at source.

	£	£
Personal allowance		3,005
Married couple's allowance		1,720
		4,725
Less car benefit for 2200cc car less than four years old (minimum miles 2,500 plus)	3,550	
car petrol benefit	900	
		4,450
		275
Less restriction for £58 tax underpaid from 1986/87 (taxpayer's top rate assumed to be 40%)		145
		130
Divide by 10		13

The employee's coding should therefore be 13H ('H' indicating that he is entitled to the married couple's allowance). If it differs from this he should seek an explanation from the Revenue.

It is particularly important to check that the married couple's allowance is coded in for 1990/91 where the wife's earnings election (as described in question 8) had previously applied.

Where the individual has more than one employer, his allowances and deductions are normally given against one employment only and a coding fixed accordingly. Special codings are then given for his other employments so that these are taxed at a fixed rate, estimated to recover more or less the right amount of tax in total over the tax year.

Where there is a change in the overall level of allowances, for example an increase in the single person's or married couple's allowances (see questions 7 and 9), the Inland Revenue will advise employers on a block basis as to how much their employees' codings should be changed by (the coding includes an identifying letter, such as 'H' used in the example above, to enable this to be done). Therefore, an individual employee need not take any action. There is usually some time lag in bringing the new codings into operation; thus for 1990/91, although the new personal allowances were announced on 20 March 1990, they will not actually take effect until the first pay day after 17 May. As described in question 27, because of the cumulative principle the changes will then be retrospective to the beginning of the tax year, 6 April 1990.

34 I have always lived in this country but part of my work is now done abroad: can I claim any tax relief?

You are now entering into the complicated areas of *domicile* and *residence* and it is important for you to have a basic understanding of these terms before the reliefs available for work done abroad are explained. However, what follows in this section is simplified and some matters are mentioned only briefly.

Generally, your *domicile* is the country you think of as your natural homeland, which is normally that of your origin at birth. It is possible to change your domicile to one of your choice, but only if you sever all connections with the country of your origin and demonstrate firm evidence of your intention to settle permanently in the other country.

Once it is known in what country you are domiciled, your *residence status* has to be decided for a tax year as this can decide how much of your earnings are taxed for that year, as you will see later. There are three terms involved here – resident, ordinarily resident and not resident. *Resident* and *not resident* are factual terms meaning, as you would expect, that you are either living in this country at the time or you are not. The term *ordinarily resident* refers to someone who normally or habitually lives in this country, although he may be abroad at the present time.

Much depends on an individual's circumstances in determining his residence status, but the following general points may be helpful:

1 If an individual spends more than six months in the UK in any one tax year he will be regarded as resident in the UK, at least for that period.

2 If an ordinarily resident individual has an abode available as a place of residence in the UK, then if he sets foot in the UK at any time, even for one day, he is likely to be regarded as resident in the UK for the whole of that tax year.

This rule is *not* applied if the individual is working abroad full time in employment or self-employment.

3 If an individual comes to the UK to work and intends to stay for at least two years, he will be treated as resident here from the date of his arrival to the date of his departure.

4 An individual who comes to work in the UK will become ordinarily resident from the beginning of the tax year following the third anniversary of his arrival.

5 If an individual comes to the UK with the intention at the outset of staying for more than three years, he will be treated as ordinarily resident here from the date of his arrival.

6 An individual who spends an average of more than three months in each tax year over a four year period in this country is likely to be treated as ordinarily resident thereafter.

7 A wife's residence status can be looked at separately to that of her husband and they may, in appropriate circumstances, be treated as separate individuals for these purposes, unless it is to their disadvantage.

8 Because the tests for residence for tax purposes differ between countries, many double taxation agreements (see question 26) contain special rules to prevent individuals being treated as resident in both countries at the same time.

The following reliefs apply to an individual who is *domiciled, resident* and *ordinarily resident* in the UK.

Where the duties of an employment are performed wholly or partly outside the UK and the time spent abroad is at least 365 days, there is no UK tax on these earnings; this is referred to as the *100% deduction*. There are provisions relaxing the 365 day requirement when time spent in this country does not exceed 62 consecutive days or one-sixth of the time elapsed since the first day of absence. The deduction is only available against the earnings in respect of work performed abroad (i.e. earnings relating to work done in this country will be fully taxable).

Travelling expenses to and from an overseas employment are not taxable where these are met by the employer; also tax free are board and lodging and expenses of travelling between different overseas employments. Costs of travel for wife and children may also be included under certain conditions.

If you are leaving the country to work abroad you are required to complete a questionnaire for the Revenue (form P85) so that a ruling can be made as to your residence status. Where the employer is resident in the UK he will operate PAYE in the usual way (see question 27). Where it is clear that the 100% deduction will apply, a special coding is issued so that the employer may pay the relevant remuneration without deducting tax.

Generally, where these deductions are claimed, the Inland Revenue are likely to scrutinise the arrangements to ensure that the remuneration paid is reasonable in relation to the duties performed and, in particular, that there is no 'loading' of remuneration against which a deduction is claimed as compared with that against which no deduction applies.

Now turning to the taxation of a *non-resident*, the basic rule is that a non-resident's employment earnings are taxed in the UK only insofar as they are attributable to any duties of that employment which are performed in this country. In instances where duties are carried out partly in this country and partly overseas, separate contracts of employment are strongly recommended. If duties are normally performed overseas, any duties performed in this country will still be treated as if they were performed overseas provided they are merely *incidental* to the overseas duties. In general, in determining whether or not duties are 'incidental', it is not the time spent in this country which is the deciding factor; on the other hand, if the duties in this country occupy more than three months in a tax year, they cannot normally be said to be incidental. The Revenue will take into account the nature of the duties and their relationship to the overseas duties. (Again, remember that if any of the income is taxed in both countries it may be possible to claim double taxation relief – see question 26.) Personal allowances for UK income tax are basically only available to a UK resident, but certain categories of non-residents may also be entitled to claim them.

35 I have always lived abroad but now I have come to work in the UK: what is my tax position?

If you were born abroad and have always lived in that country your 'domicile' will generally be your country of origin as explained in

63

the previous question. If you are *not domiciled in the UK but are resident and ordinarily resident* in this country (i.e. you are living here for six months or more in a tax year and you habitually live in this country), the general rules as to paying income tax are as follows: any income arising within the UK is chargeable to tax in full, any income arising outside the UK is chargeable to tax only by reference to the amounts which are remitted to the UK.

If the *employer is resident abroad and you, the employee, are domiciled abroad* your residence status may affect the way your earnings from that employer are taxed. If you are *resident and ordinarily resident* in the UK and have been since before 13 March 1984, *and* your job with the non-resident employer began before that date, then for years up to 1986/87, tax was only charged on 50% of those earnings; for 1987/88 and 1988/89 this deduction was reduced to 25% and thereafter withdrawn altogether. Moreover it did *not* apply in 1984/85 or later years if you had been resident in the UK for at least nine out of the ten preceding years.

The deduction was not available at all if your job with the non-resident employer did not begin until after 13 March 1984, unless you took up duty in the UK before 1 August 1984 under a posting which had already been arranged on or before 13 March 1984.

These rules do not apply to individuals who are employed by an employer resident in the Republic of Ireland; their earnings are specifically excluded from the relief.

A person who is resident in the UK may claim the personal allowances discussed in earlier questions.

3 NOW YOU ARE IN BUSINESS

TAXATION OF THE SELF-EMPLOYED

36 What happens when I start up in business?

Special rules apply for taxation purposes when a business first commences and when it ceases, otherwise tax would not be paid until a business was well under way, and would also be payable some time after it had ceased. Because of these rules tax savings are possible, if matters are timed correctly and the accounting date is chosen with care (see question 40).

It is important to determine the actual date on which a business commences as this also decides the first assessment for tax purposes. *The first assessment will tax the actual profits from the date the business started to the next 5 April* (i.e. end of the tax year). This will most probably mean the assessment is made on a proportion of the profits shown in the first accounts (computed on a time basis).

The second assessment will tax the profits of the first 12 months trading, from the date of commencement; however if the first accounts are for a period of *less* than 12 months, the second and third years assessments will also be made on a time basis (which would most probably mean a proportion of the profit from the first two sets of accounts). If the *first accounts were prepared for a 12 month period* the third year's assessment will be based on the first accounts. This is called the *previous year basis of assessment* and will continue throughout the period of self-employment until the final year (see question 42), so that the profit of your accounting period *ending* in the tax year 1989/90 will actually be *taxed* in 1990/91.

You do have an option that *all* the first three years of assessment be taxed on the actual profits for those years. This is only to be done if it is to your advantage (i.e. if the figures are smaller than those produced by the normal basis) and the election will normally only be made if the profits of the second and third accounting periods are lower than those earned in the first year of trading.

Claims must be made within six years from the end of the third year of assessment.

If this election is not advantageous the first accounting period will be the basis for the first three years' tax assessments, so it is important that the tax profits be kept as low as possible. You should consult your professional adviser as to how this may be properly achieved.

In the following questions, general reference is made to 'trades' and 'trading', but exactly the same considerations are given to an individual carrying on a *profession* or *vocation*.

● **37   What can I claim as expenses?**

Many people who are self-employed do not realise that the profit appearing in their accounts is not necessarily the same figure that will be assessed to tax. The accounts profit has to be adjusted for tax purposes as not all the expenses shown in the accounts are tax allowable. The basic rule is that *expenses are allowable if they are incurred wholly and exclusively for the purposes of the trade.* Thus it follows that if an expense was incurred partly for private purposes the whole of the expenditure will be disallowed as it does not fulfil the criterion of being wholly and exclusively for business purposes.

It would not be possible to set out all the allowable or disallowable expenses and your professional advisers will be able to tell you what you can or cannot claim. You must ensure that all the expenses you have incurred during a year are included in your accounts otherwise you may pay more tax than is necessary. Below is a list of some of the items most frequently seen in statements of expenses, with an indication as to what may or may not be allowable expenditure for tax purposes.

Depreciation: Not allowable, but capital allowances may be claimed instead (see question 38).

Advertising: Generally allowable.

Remuneration: Allowable including bonuses, PAYE, cost of benefits provided to employees, but *not to the proprietor*.

Entertainment expenses: Not allowable, unless for staff. Before 16

March 1988, deduction was allowed for entertaining overseas customers but this has now been withdrawn. Disallowance similarly applies for VAT purposes: for overseas customers from 1 August 1988 (see question 97).

Legal fees: Not allowable if incurred while acquiring a new asset as this is part of the capital cost. Generally allowable if it is the cost of maintaining existing trading assets and rights (e.g. debt collecting).

Personal expenses: Not allowable.

Rent, rates, etc., for business purposes: Allowable, but note that the *personal community charge* (otherwise known as the 'poll tax') payable by the individual proprietor is always regarded as a personal expense of his and not deductible for tax purposes. Where the proprietor pays the charge on behalf of any of his employees it will then be deductible to him as a business expense but taxable on the employees as a benefit in kind (see question 30).

Employee training: The costs of training staff in connection with their job are generally allowable. In particular, contributions by businesses to support *training and enterprise councils* (TECs) and *local enterprise agencies* (LEAs) are specifically deductible up to 1 April 1995.

Income tax and NIC: Allowable on employees' pay, not allowable in relation to employer's personal liabilities.

Subscriptions: Allowable if to trade or professional association or for trade publications.

Donations: Donations to charities are allowable provided the 'wholly and exclusively' rule is satisfied (i.e. there is a demonstrable business connection).

Travelling and subsistence: Allowable if in the course of the business activities. Not allowable are travelling expenses between home and the place of business (as in question 32).

Repairs and renewals: Expenditure on additions, alterations or improvements is capital and not allowable. Repairs (i.e. restoring something to its original condition, etc.) are allowable. Expenditure on preparing and making good landfill sites for waste disposal is specifically allowable for tax purposes from 6 April 1989.

Leasing: Generally allowable in full where assets used wholly and exclusively for business purposes. Exceptionally a restriction is applied for motor cars costing more than £8,000 when new.

Telephone: Business use only allowable.

Where any such expenditure is incurred in connection with a new business in the five years prior to the commencement of trading, it may also be claimed as a deduction in the first year's tax assessment.

You will appreciate it is easier for a self-employed person to claim expenses in respect of his work than for an employee, whose claim may fail on the grounds it is not a 'necessary' expense (see question 32).

Some years ago, considerable interest was aroused in a case where a lady barrister tried to claim a deduction for tax purposes for the special dark clothes that she was required to wear in court. Eventually the House of Lords ruled against her on the grounds that she was not able to establish that she had bought the clothes concerned *exclusively* for the purposes of her profession: she also had to meet the personal requirements of decency and warmth!

It should be noted that small businesses, ie those with a turnover of less than £10,000 a year, are no longer required to send in detailed accounts to the Revenue. With effect from April 1990 a simple three line account, showing total turnover, total business expenses and the resulting net profit, is all that will normally be required. The trader will still need to keep accurate business records.

38 What is the effect for tax purposes of capital expenditure?

If you incur expenditure in acquiring a capital asset you may not deduct this from your trading profit. Assuming that the asset has a limited life span, its value to your business will gradually decline and this is anticipated by including in the accounts an amount for depreciation, but this in itself is not allowable for tax purposes. Instead there are specific allowances available in respect of specific capital expenditure, as noted below.

Machinery and plant
Industrial buildings
Agricultural land and buildings
Mines, oil wells and mineral deposits
Dredging
Scientific research
Patents
Know-how
Cemeteries

The first three of these categories (being the most common) are dealt with in more detail below.

It may be that a particular item of capital expenditure falls into more than one category and you would normally be able to state your preference which will obviously be to your advantage, but there are special provisions which restrict this choice in certain contexts. You must make a claim to the Revenue for the allowances but you will see it is not always advantageous to claim them. In general, the granting of the allowances falls into three categories.

1 An *initial or first year allowance* of a substantial percentage of the capital expenditure. These allowances have been largely phased out so as to apply no longer for expenditure incurred after 31 March 1986 and they are therefore not considered further in this book.

2 A *writing down allowance* each year during the life of the asset; again, this may be claimed in part if desired.

3 A *balancing charge or allowance* at the end of the trade or on the disposal of the asset. This will bring the allowances given into line with the actual amount spent, i.e. the difference between original cost and the proceeds of disposal: if the amount given by way of allowances is less than the amount spent the difference is a *balancing allowance*; if the allowances given exceed the amount spent, the difference is brought into the income tax assessment by way of a *balancing charge*. (If the asset is sold at an overall profit the amount brought back into charge will not exceed the original allowances given: the excess may be charged to CGT – see Chapter 5.)

The allowance is normally set against your taxable profits but if you have a loss the capital allowances can be used to increase the loss or they can be applied so as to turn a profit into a loss. A word of advice – remember you cannot carry forward your personal allowances and you must consider whether or not you wish to claim the full capital allowances (for treatment of losses see question 43 and 44).

Machinery and plant

This is certainly the most common of the capital allowances claims. As there is no definition of machinery or plant in the legislation it has provoked much discussion through the years. It includes *fixtures and fittings* but recently the Revenue has been taking a much stricter view as to what qualifies; it depends on the relation of the fixture in the building and whether or not it is used for the trade. One example is where special lighting and wall decorations were installed in a number of pubs to improve the atmosphere. It was held that because of the contribution that these fittings made to the development of business, they could be treated as fixtures and fittings and so qualify for capital allowances, rather than as part of the 'setting' (which would not qualify) in which the trade was carried out.

The terms 'machinery' and 'plant' also include *motor vehicles* and these are dealt with in question 39.

All plant and machinery used in the trade is grouped together into a 'pool' (but see question 39 regarding motor vehicles). For the first year it is claimed, a *writing down* allowance is given of 25% of the cost. The net figure of the cost less the allowance is called the *written down value* – in the following year an allowance is given of 25% of this figure and the same procedure is repeated in subsequent years.

Industrial buildings

General rules are as follows:
1 Building must be an industrial building or structure – defined in great detail in the legislation.
2 Claimant may be a trader or a landlord, but the expenditure *must* be incurred on the construction of 'an industrial building or structure which is to be occupied *for the purposes of a trade*'.
3 Cost of land is excluded; private roads are included by concession.
4 Special rules where only part of the building qualifies, where expenditure was incurred before 1962 and when the building is sold.

5 Special rules and allowances for hotels and for commercial buildings in *enterprise zones*.
6 *Writing down allowance* of 4% of cost until fully written off (i.e. after 25 years).

Agricultural land and buildings

General rules are as follows:
1 Expenditure must be incurred for husbandry – proportion of the allowance may be given where appropriate.
2 Claimant may be the landlord or tenant of any agricultural land who incurs expenditure on construction of farmhouses, farm buildings, cottages, fences or other works (e.g. water supplies, drainage).
3 Apportionment of allowance applies when expenditure is on a farmhouse – one-third is normally allowable.
4 Special rules apply when the building is sold.
5 *Writing down allowance* at 4% of cost until fully written off (i.e. after 25 years).

39 What is the tax position of buying motor cars? If I use my own car can I claim tax allowances?

As you have already seen, motor vehicles are classed as plant and machinery but only certain types qualify as 'machinery and plant' so as to be included in the 'pool' described in question 38. These are goods vehicles (e.g. lorries), vehicles unsuitable to be used as private vehicles (or not commonly used as such) and vehicles which are provided wholly or mainly for hire to the general public.

Otherwise a motor car does qualify for the 25% writing down allowance but it must be included in a separate 'pool' from other machinery and plant. Further, if the car cost more than £8,000, the writing down allowance is restricted to £2,000 each year, until the amount brought forward falls below £8,000 when the 25% rate of allowance becomes applicable.

If all the car expenses have been claimed in the accounts and these include private motoring expenses, an adjustment will be made to the taxable profit as you are not entitled to tax relief for the private use of your car. If you use your own car for business purposes, you may claim the writing down allowance and running expenses but only in proportion to the business use. Finally, remember that when the car is sold (whether it is owned by the business or yourself), if you have been claiming writing down allowances, an adjustment will be made in the form of a balancing allowance or charge as explained in question 38.

● **40 How do I choose my accounting date?**

Most people when left to their own devices will automatically prepare accounts for the first twelve months trading without seeking further advice: admittedly this has one advantage in enabling the first three years' tax assessments to be settled earlier, but that is all. Other people prepare accounts for the calendar year or even the tax year. You should always consult a professional adviser before you decide on your accounting date as there may be an advantage in choosing a particular date depending on the line of business you are in. As a general guide, the date that has the most advantages is one early in the tax year (e.g. 30 April). You must remember that the choice of your accounting date is not a way of saving tax, but rather one of deferring payment of that tax, and this is brought about by the operation of the preceding year basis of assessment mentioned in the previous question.

As you have seen, the basis of assessment means that the profits you make during one year will not be taxed until the following year. To illustrate the point, the examples below use two different accounting dates – 30 September and 30 April.

Examples

Ivor Crown, a dentist, makes up his accounts to 30 September.
Accounts to *30 September 1990*
Profits taxable in 1991/92
Payment dates for tax in equal instalments:
1 January 1992
1 July 1992
The time lapse between the end of the accounting period and the due date of payment of the first instalment is *15 months*.

Orson Carte, a rag-and-bone man, makes up his accounts to 30 April.
Accounts to *30 April 1990*
Profits taxable in 1991/92

Payment dates for tax in equal instalments:
1 January 1992
1 July 1992
The time lapse between the end of the accounting period and the
due date of payment of the first instalment is *20 months*. Mr Carte
therefore has 5 months extra time between the end of the accounting period and the due dates of payment. As pointed out previously, it will not save him tax but it may help his cash flow
situation. (Refer to question 2 for details of when tax liabilities
become due for payment.)

41   What happens if I change my accounting date?

If you are already in business and have a year end you think may
not be giving you the best tax break, you may wish to consider
changing your accounting date – no general advice can be given as
each case *must* be examined separately. In many cases it may *not*
be worthwhile because a change of accounting date means the
basis of assessment of your profits is affected and may result in
increased tax liabilities; before any change is made it is essential to
make detailed calculations for which you will require up-to-date
accounts and accurate forecasts of trading, stock levels, etc.

   If your profits have been reasonably static but an increase is
likely in the future, it maybe possible to obtain some saving of tax
if you can move your accounting date from *late* in the tax year to
early in the year. On the other hand, if profits have been high in
the past and are now falling there may be scope for shortening the
accounting period, especially if the original accounting date fell
early in the tax year. The tax savings for this sort of venture may
be large enough to make it a worthwhile exercise.

42   What happens if my business ceases?

The actual date of cessation is important (as for commencing in
business) as this determines the final year of assessment. If you
permanently discontinue your trade, the profits assessed in the
final tax year are the *actual* profits earned from the start of that tax
year (i.e. 6 April) to the date of cessation. You may remember
that *you* had the option at the outset as to what was assessed in the

second and third years of assessment – this time *the Revenue* have the option to revise the previous two years' assessments (i.e. the two years before the final year, which have otherwise both been assessed on a previous year basis) to assess the *profits actually earned* during the periods, calculated on a time basis. The Revenue will elect to do this if the total profits to be assessed on an 'actual' basis exceed the profits using the 'preceding year' basis.

Whichever basis is used, part of your profits will actually not be assessed at all but this is counteracted by the fact that your initial trading profits will have been assessed more than once.

The timing of the cessation is important; each case requires careful consideration of its particular facts and an accurate estimate of profits to the date you propose to cease trading. A general rule is that where profits are falling the trade should cease prior to the start of the new tax year, but if profits are still rising it may be beneficial to cease early in the following tax year. In addition, there are special provisions relating to capital allowances (see question 38).

● 43 What can I do if I incur a loss in the first years of trading?

If you should be unfortunate enough to make a loss during any of the first four years of assessment from the date the trade commenced, you may make a claim that this loss be set off against your *other* income for the preceding three years, using the earlier years first, so allowing you to reduce or reclaim tax arising for those earlier years. The Revenue will want you to show that the trade was carried on during the period the loss arose on a *commercial basis* with an expectation of profits in the near future, and you must make your claim within two years of the end of the year of assessment in which the loss occurred.

Otherwise, loss relief may be claimed under one of the ways described in question 44. Under certain circumstances it may be possible to use a combination of these reliefs.

● 44 What other ways are there of relieving losses?

If a loss has been sustained by you *at any time* in the trade you are carrying on, this may be utilised in one of the following ways.

1 Set off losses against other income: A trading loss may be set off against your other income in the same year of assessment or in the following year of assessment provided that the trade is still carried on in the later year.

A claim must be made within two years of the end of the year of assessment in question and the loss must be set off against your other earned income, followed by your unearned income. Repayment of tax is then made accordingly. Up to 5 April 1990, it was also possible to set losses against your spouse's earned and unearned income, if your own was used up, but with the introduction of independent taxation (see question 9) this facility was withdrawn for loss claims arising after that date.

It is possible to increase your loss by claiming capital allowances, but in any event no loss relief will be given unless the trade was carried on for the year in question on a commercial basis with a view to realising a profit.

2 Carry-forward of losses against subsequent years' profits: If you claim relief under the above provisions you will receive the immediate benefit of a tax repayment, but you may decide it would be more beneficial to carry all your losses forward to a later year to be set against future profits from the *same trade*. You may claim your loss relief either by setting off the loss against your other income for the year, or carrying back the loss if it was incurred in the first years of trading, but you may still have a balance – this may be carried forward instead of the full amount. There is generally no time limit as to how many years the loss can be carried forward until it is completely used up, provided only that the same trade is still being carried on.

3 Carry-back of a terminal loss: A *terminal loss* is the amount of losses sustained in the *last 12 months of trading* when your business was permanently discontinued. These losses may be carried back and set off against the profits of your trade for the three years immediately prior to that in which the cessation occurred. Relief is given for the latest year first, then working backwards until the loss or the available profit is used up.

Beware of forfeiting your personal allowances. If your other income is low for the year in which you have a loss it may be covered by personal allowances. If this is the case do not claim for the loss to be used that year but carry it forward.

Remember, you can carry your losses forward but you *cannot* carry your personal allowances forward.

● 45 As a self-employed person, what provision can I make towards my retirement?

As indicated in question 16, fundamental changes have been made in the area of pensions and pension provision and these substantially affect the position of *self-employed* individuals.

Up to 30 June 1988, such individuals were entitled to enter into *retirement annuity premium* (RAP) policies with insurance companies which would provide them with a pension, normally between the ages of 60 and 75, with the option of commuting a part of that pension for a tax-free capital sum at retirement, the amount of which would be dependent on the individual's age then. This arrangement was also open to individuals in non-pensionable employment (i.e. for whom there is no approved company scheme, as described in question 16, available).

If you have entered into such an arrangement, you may be entitled to deduct from your 'net relevant earnings' as assessed for a tax year, any premium paid under a Revenue approved annuity contract. The term *net relevant earnings* means your earnings from your self-employment (or non-pensionable employment) having taken into account losses and capital allowances.

You are allowed to claim a certain percentage of your net relevant earnings as a qualifying premium, depending on when you were born. Currently the rates are as follows.

Age at beginning of tax year	Percentage
Under 51	17.5
51–55	20
56–60	22.5
60 or over	27.5

Out of the above percentages, you can contribute up to 5% of net relevant earnings to provide for the payment of a lump sum on your death before retirement.

This relief will normally be given against income in the tax year in which the premium is paid, but it is possible to elect for a premium to be treated as paid in the previous tax year, or if there were no relevant earnings in that year, in the next preceding tax year.

It may also be possible to make use of 'unused relief' from earlier years. Where the maximum amount of relief which would be available exceeds the premium paid in a year, the excess is to be treated as unused relief: this may be carried forward for up to six years and used when the reverse situation arises and the premiums paid exceed the amount allowable. Relief given in this way must be taken in the earliest possible year and the full amount of relief due for that year must be taken up first. *In general*, the rule to remember is that it is possible to take up unused relief before the end of six years, but that it is lost when the six year period comes to an end. However, it is possible by using the 'relating back' rules mentioned above to obtain an extension. For instance, unused relief for 1983/84, should strictly be forfeited by 5 April 1990 but if a payment were to be made in the following year, 1990/91, it could be related back to 1989/90 and then unused relief for 1983/84 could be set against any excess premiums in that year.

Although no new RAP policies could be entered into after 30 June 1988, it is still open to self-employed individuals to continue to pay premiums into such schemes so as to build up their pension entitlement: this is, of course, wholly dependent on the amounts paid in.

From 1 July 1988, it has also been possible to make pension provision through a *personal pension plan* (PPP). This is similar in concept in many ways to RAP arrangements, particularly as regards relating back premiums to the previous tax year (or possibly to the one before that) and the carry forward of unused relief for up to six years. There are a number of significant differences, however, as noted below:

(1) As indicated in question 16, an individual in employment may withdraw from his employer's approved pension scheme (or decide not to join it) and instead set up a PPP. The pros and cons are discussed in question 16.

(2) Under a PPP, a pension may be drawn at age 50 (instead of 60).

(3) The tax-free commutation is fixed at 25% of the accumulated fund irrespective of the individual's age at that time; this is likely to be less than that available under a RAP policy.

(4) The percentage of net relevant earnings allowed are as follows:

Age at beginning of tax year	Percentage
Under 36	17.5
36–45	20
46–50	25
51–55	30
56–60	35
61 or over	40

(5) The percentage limits mentioned in (4) only apply to net relevant earnings up to a limit initially set for 1989/90 at £60,000 so that it is not possible to contribute in respect of earnings over that level. This limit is to be adjusted annually in line with the retail prices index: thus for 1990/91 it has been fixed at £64,800. This restriction may make these plans less attractive to high earners than RAP schemes.

One other aspect of interest is the 'loan-back' facility. In the past, one of the disadvantages of paying into a pension scheme was the fact that money was paid in and was not seen again until the date of retirement. Facilities are now offered by a number of life assurance companies which allow you to borrow back an amount up to the level of the premiums paid; this means that the only cost need be the interest on the loan, which is charged at a commercial rate. The loan will be repaid when the policy matures, either out of the funds of the pension itself or your own personal funds.

This is a complex area and if you are concerned about providing for your retirement you should seek specialist independent advice.

46 Are there any businesses which have special rules?

No matter what trade, profession or vocation you are engaged in, you will find differences, particularly in relation to the expenses which are allowable, but there are certain categories which are set apart in the legislation for special treatment. Three of these categories are discussed very briefly below.

1 Subcontractors in the construction industry: The main thing to remember in this instance is that unless you hold a *subcontractor's exemption certificate* (form 714) you will have basic rate tax deducted from all the payments you receive for your work. This tax is then available as a credit when an agreement concerning your tax is eventually reached, so the main disadvantage is with regard to your cash flow situation, which could be of major importance. In order to obtain an exemption certificate, you must keep all your income tax returns, accounts and payments of tax up to date as all these things are examined closely before the issue of a certificate is authorised; some of these requirements may be relaxed in the case of school or college leavers who are newly starting in the industry.

2 Farmers: Basically the rules of assessment are the same as for any other self-employed person but there are a few notable differences:

Losses – unlike other trades, all farming (but not market gardening) is treated as *one* trade so that a loss on one farm may be set off against the profit on another. However, it is not possible to set farming losses against other income for the same year or a succeeding year of assessment (see question 44) if losses were also incurred in farming in each of the five years preceding the year of assessment concerned, except in certain circumstances.

Treatment of livestock – generally animals kept by a farmer are to be treated as trading stock. Where animals such as these form part of a production herd the farmer may elect for them to be treated as a capital asset – the so-called *herd basis*. (If you think this applies to your livestock – seek further advice).

Fluctuating profits – complicated rules apply, but a good way of saving tax if the tests are met. Relief is by way of averaging two successive years' profits where there is a difference between the two years of more than 25% of the higher figure.

3 Landowners: Landowners who are not carrying on a trade are taxed on rent less expenses and this net figure is treated as unearned income, unless they meet the special tests relating to *furnished holiday accommodation* (see question 26). There are also what are called 'one estate' provisions in that expenses incurred on one property may be set against the rents arising on another within the same 'estate' provided that certain conditions are satisfied.

47 What is the position if I am in partnership?

First of all it must be shown that there is actually a partnership: *an agreement to trade together and share the profits or losses* is presumed to be a partnership. The agreement does not have to be a formal legal document (in fact it can be made orally), but it is preferable to have the terms written down in some form.

Where there is a partnership, income tax is assessed on the profits of the trade or profession in the name of the partnership, although in England and Wales a partnership is not a legal entity. *Each partner is jointly liable for income tax on the whole of the partnership's profits.* Where a partnership includes a company, special rules are needed because a company, unlike an individual, is always taxed on the current year's profits, i.e. no preceding year basis of assessment.

The rules concerning the allocation of profits of a partnership are rather involved. The partners agree for each accounting year how the accounts profit is to be divided between them – this is called the *profit sharing ratio*. However, the same profit is not necessarily divided up in the same way for tax purposes. This is because the profit sharing ratio for the purposes of the income tax assessment is the ratio actually in use for that tax year and due to the preceding year basis of assessment the accounts profits for one year are not assessed until the following year, by which time the partners may have agreed to allocate their current profits differently; this is illustrated in the following example.

Example

John, Paul and Peter are in partnership. They make up their accounts to 31 March each year. The accounts to 31 March 1990 show a taxable profit of £72,000 which is divided *equally* between them. This profit will be taxed in 1990/91 (the tax year ended 5 April 1991).

Shortly after the start of their new accounting period it is decided that because John works so hard he is to have one-half of the current year's profit (to 31 March 1991) while Paul and Peter will now take only one-quarter each.

The income tax assessment for 1990/91 is based on the profits to 31 March 1990 (£72,000) but it is divided using the profit sharing ratio for the current year, i.e. to 31 March 1991. The assessment is therefore divided up as follows.

Taxable profit £72,000   John – £36,000
                          Paul – £18,000
                          Peter – £18,000

However, each partner is actually entitled to £24,000 for the year concerned. It may be possible to turn this sort of situation to your advantage with careful planning and professional advice.

Partners' salaries and interest on capital are not an allowable expense for income tax purposes, being regarded as an allocation of the partnership profits.

48 What happens if there is a change in the partnership?

In the event of any change in the partners, for tax purposes the business is automatically assumed to have ceased and a new business started at the date of the change: this brings into operation special provisions relating to commencement and cessation. So far as the 'old partnership' is concerned, the rules described in question 42 apply. As regards the 'new partnership', up to 19 March 1985 the provisions set out in question 36 applied; for partnership changes taking place after that date, the partnership is assessed to tax on its actual profits for the first *four* years with the normal previous year basis only applying in the fifth and subsequent years. There is still an option to have the fifth and sixth years assessed on an actual basis if this is to the partners' advantage.

But if there is one partner (at least) who is a partner both before and after the change it is possible to elect for the *continuing basis of assessment* to apply. The election must be signed by all the partners both before and after the change (or, in the case of a deceased partner, by an executor) and the claim *must* be made within two years of the date of the change – it can also be revoked during this time. It must be emphasised that the Revenue are very strict in the application of this particular time limit.

The effect of the election will be for the profits to be assessed on the normal preceding year basis, the year of change being apportioned between the 'old' and 'new' partnerships on a time basis.

It is often beneficial to make the election and the necessary calculations should always be made to ensure that as little tax as possible is payable. It is essential to seek professional advice on this matter.

● **49 Part of my business is carried on abroad: can I claim any tax deduction for this?**

Generally, profits arising from self-employed trade or professional earnings are charged to UK tax in full, irrespective of where they arise.

However, where a separate part of the business activities are carried on abroad, such that they are demonstrably managed and controlled outside the UK, some relief from UK tax may be available to certain categories of partner. Those who *are not domiciled* though *resident* in this country will be liable to tax only on *remittances* of income to the UK from the overseas business. Partners who are *not resident and not ordinarily resident* in the UK will not be liable to UK tax on such earnings.

● **50 Should I consider turning my business into a company?**

There may be a number of non-tax reasons why incorporation is attractive, for example an incorporated entity may provide some personal protection against product liability claims. On the other hand, incorporation does not always give effective protection of limited liability (e.g. where a personal guarantee has to be given to a bank).

You should first of all consult with your professional adviser to discuss what would be the most suitable form of trading vehicle for your particular business. The reduction in income tax rates since the 1970s, and the higher level of NICs payable by employer and employee compared with the contributions paid by the self-employed (see question 17 and Appendix 4), have made the decision to incorporate less clear cut.

Let us look at the main advantages and disadvantages in more detail.

Advantages

1 You would be able to establish a company pension scheme (subject to approval by the Inland Revenue). The contributions paid by the company and the employee are tax deductible and may be greater than the amounts allowable for personal pension or retirement annuity premiums (see questions 16 and 45). The benefits may also be more attractive.

2 You may be able to make gifts of shares to utilise the annual inheritance tax exemptions (see question 88). The capital gains tax position should not be overlooked but it may be possible to keep the chargeable gain below the taxable limit or take advantage of the holdover relief available for certain gifts (see question 74).

3 It may be easier for you to raise additional finance from banks and other third parties.

4 The benefit of limited liability can be obtained which can give valuable protection against financial and other risks.

Disadvantages

1 Additional accounting and audit requirements are imposed on companies.

2 You may lose some of the flexibility of your previous business arrangements. You will be required to maintain minutes of directors and shareholders meetings and to comply with the statutory filing requirements, the most important one being to file a copy of the accounts with the Companies Registration Office each year. Such filed accounts are available for inspection by any member of the public.

3 Once you become a director of a company rather than a participant in an unincorporated business (whether by yourself or in partnership) you are then subject to the stricter rules concerning benefits and expenses, and your drawings from the company are subject to PAYE – which can cause cash flow problems.

4 If you have a husband and wife partnership with a flexible profit sharing agreement this will have to cease if the business is incorporated. The agreement may have meant your spouse was given a material slice of the profits to utilise personal allowances and the lower rates of tax, although he or she perhaps did not take a very active part in the business. Once the business becomes a company any remuneration paid will be reviewed more critically by the Inland Revenue (as described in question 10) and if it is considered to be excessive for the duties actually undertaken, the Inspector may seek to disallow a part of the salary paid for corporation tax purposes.

● 51 How does incorporation affect my income tax position?

The transfer of your business to a company is treated as a cessation of the unincorporated business and the special rules for the final years of trading will apply (see question 42). The timing of the incorporation therefore requires careful planning if increased income tax assessments are to be avoided. There are special rules concerning capital allowances and losses. These are complicated but can be used to produce some saving in tax.

4 KEEPING GOOD COMPANY

TAXATION OF THE COMPANY – CORPORATION TAX

52   What are the basic rules of corporation tax (including rates of tax, reliefs, dates for payments, etc.)?

The first and perhaps the most obvious rule is that corporation tax is only paid by companies. A company means any *body corporate or unincorporated association* but does not include a partnership, a local authority or a local authority association. There are special rules and exemptions for certain types of companies, such as charitable companies, unregistered friendly societies, trade unions and scientific research associations.

To be liable to pay corporation tax a company must be *resident* in the UK and it will then pay tax on all its profits, wherever they arise. The basic rule is that any company *incorporated in the UK* on or after 15 March 1988 will automatically be resident in the UK for taxation purposes, with the consequences described above.

Companies incorporated in the UK before 15 March 1988 but managed and controlled on a day-to-day basis outside the UK may still be able to rely on that criterion for defining residence so as to be held to be non-resident for up to five years from that date. If the seat of central management and control is transferred to the UK before 14 March 1993, the company will become resident at the date of transfer; otherwise this will happen automatically at the latter date. *Non-resident* companies are only subject to corporation tax if they are carrying on a trade through a branch or agency in the UK, and then only on the profits arising from that branch or agency. See also question 64.

Unlike income tax assessments on individuals and sole traders, corporation tax is not complicated by the preceding year basis of assessment. Corporation tax is assessed on a company for its *accounting period*. The accounting period for tax purposes is normally the same as the company's period of account: it is sometimes necessary to determine an accounting period in instances where the company commences or ceases to trade during a period of account, or the period of account is longer than a year. An accounting period for tax purposes *cannot* exceed 12 months, so where the company prepares its accounts for a period of more than 12 months there will be two accounting periods, one for 12 months and the other for the balance, the profits being allocated on a time basis. If, therefore, the company has an 18 month period of account, there will be an assessment raised on the first 12 months on two-thirds of the profit and a further assessment for the other six months on one-third of the profit.

Corporation tax is charged, not for the income tax year ended 5 April, but for the *financial year to 31 March*. If an accounting period straddles that date, the profits have to be apportioned between two financial years and taxed accordingly.

The rates of corporation tax currently fixed are 35% for the years ended 31 March 1990 and 1991. These rates apply where the annual profits exceed £1 million for 1991, £750,000 for 1990.

A *small companies rate* applies where the annual profits do not exceed £200,000 for 1991, £150,000 for 1990; this has been set at 25% for the years ended 31 March 1990 and 1991. There is a marginal relief available where the profits fall between £250,000 and £1 million for 1991, £150,000 and £750,000 for 1990.

The tax is normally due nine months after the end of the accounting period, or if the assessment is made late, within 30 days of the date the assessment is issued.

If the tax is paid late the risk is run of incurring an *interest charge* as for income tax (see question 5), but on the other hand if there is a corporation tax refund due from the Inland Revenue, if certain tests are satisfied there may be a *repayment supplement* due, again with similar rules to income tax.

You may have heard the term *close company* which is applied to a company that is controlled by five (or fewer) shareholders or by its directors. (This is over-simplifying the position – the rules to decide whether a company is close or not are very complicated.) Formerly, the legislation was such that if a company was close it could lead to problems as the law required a certain amount of the income of these companies to be distributed each year, and there was also a much wider definition of what constituted a distribution by the company. However, these provisions now only apply to certain types of investment holding companies and do not generally apply to trading companies.

53 What are the profits of a company for corporation tax purposes?

The *profits* of a company include both *income* and *chargeable gains*. The amount of income is, in general, computed in accordance with income tax principles as described in questions 37 to 39. The taxation of chargeable gains is dealt with separately (see question 57).

A company is not entitled to personal reliefs and allowances as these are only available to individuals.

Special rules apply to what are called *charges on income* which comprise chiefly of annual interest (but not bank interest), royalties and certain charitable payments (see question 54). These are allowed as deductions against the *total profits* of the accounting period in which they are *actually paid*. Interest payable to a bank is generally treated as a trading expense and not as a charge on income.

Charges on income must be paid under deduction of income tax at the basic rate and the company must pay this tax over to the Collector of Taxes (unless a group situation applies – see question 63).

54 Can a company obtain relief for donations to charity?

Although not generally qualifying as a business expense, by specific provision in the legislation, a company may obtain relief for corporation tax purposes for payments made under a deed of covenant to a charity, similar to the relief described in question 24.

As for an individual, the term of the deed must be capable of exceeding three years. As mentioned in the previous question, the payments must be made under deduction of income tax at the basic rate which must be paid over to the Collector of Taxes. However, the charity can then reclaim this tax, so effectively receiving the covenanted payment gross; the company will in the meantime be able to claim the *gross* amount of the payments as a deduction in arriving at its corporation tax liability for the accounting period in which the payments are made. The working of this is illustrated in the following example.

Example

Scrooge Ltd covenants by deed to pay the Tiny Tim Charity an annual amount of £100 for four years.

Tiny Tim Ltd:	£
From Scrooge Ltd	75
By repayment from the Inland Revenue	25
Total income under deed	£100

Scrooge Ltd:	
To the charity £100 less tax at 25%	75
Income tax withheld, paid over to Collector of Taxes	25
	100
Corporation tax relief at 35% (say)	35
Net cost to Scrooge Ltd	£ 65

As part of the government's policy to provide further support and encouragement for charitable giving, another relief for companies (other than close companies – see question 52) has been brought in. This allows them to obtain tax relief for one-off gifts to charity, up to a maximum equal to 3% of the ordinary dividends paid by the company. This relief operates in the same way as that described for charitable covenants, with the paying company deducting basic rate income tax from the payments made and accounting for that tax to the Revenue; the charity recovers the tax as before.

The *gift aid* relief described in question 24 will also be available from 1 October 1990 to allow companies, as an alternative to the 3% of dividends scheme described above, to make single cash gifts to charities of £600 or more up to a maximum of £5 million in any accounting period. The relief will operate in the same way as for charitable deeds of covenant, so that the company will deduct income tax at the basic rate from the payment and pay this over to the Revenue: it will then get corporation tax relief on the gross amount. The charities will be able to reclaim the tax withheld from the Revenue in the usual way.

● **55 What are the rules for claiming relief for capital expenditure?**

Capital allowances may be claimed by a company in the same way as for individuals and partnerships (see question 38).

56 If my company incurs losses, how can they be utilised?

Where a trading loss arises in a company there are a number of ways in which relief for it may be obtained:

1 The trading loss may be carried forward to be set against future profits from the *same trade*.

2 Alternatively, the trading loss may be set against other profits of the same period, including chargeable gains.

3 The loss may be carried back for one year and set against profits from all sources provided the company was trading during that period.

4 Trading losses incurred by a company which is a member of a group can be passed to another member of the group (this is referred to as *group relief*: see question 63).

5 Trading losses incurred in the last 12 months of trading (i.e. a *terminal loss*) can be carried back for up to three years.

6 Allowable expenditure incurred in the five years before trading commenced may be claimed as an expense in the first accounting period.

7 Where there are charges on income (see question 53) consisting of payments made wholly and exclusively for the purposes of a trade carried on by the company, and these plus other charges on income exceed the total profits of the company, then whichever is the *smaller* of the trading charges *or* the excess of charges over profit is treated as a trading expense and so entitled to *loss relief*. Losses incurred in this way can only be carried forward, they cannot be carried back as in **3** above, but they may be eligible for 'group relief' (as in **4** above – see question 63).

57 What is the CGT position of a company?

The profits of a company which are chargeable to corporation tax include its chargeable gains after setting off its losses. For disposals of assets made on or after 17 March 1987 the gains are to be charged at the appropriate rate, i.e. the normal rate of 35% or the small companies rate of 25%, as applicable.

For disposals made before 17 March 1987 a different arrangement applied; effectively, a company paid tax on its chargeable gains at the same rate as was applicable to an individual, i.e. 30%. To achieve this only a proportion of the gains was charged to tax but always at the normal rate; thus for a corporation tax rate of

35%, six-sevenths of the gains were chargeable to tax.

If a company incurs a trading loss it may carry the losses forward against future trading profits, or the loss can be set against profits of the same accounting period, no matter what the description; a *trading loss may therefore be set off against chargeable gains of the same accounting period*. However, the reverse cannot happen – a capital loss cannot be set against trading profits but can only be set against current or future capital gains. In addition, chargeable gains cannot be used to relieve trading losses brought forward nor a terminal loss carried back (see question 56).

The rules for computing chargeable gains or allowable losses for companies are generally similar to those for individuals described in Chapter 5.

58   What are the tax consequences if my company pays a dividend?

Persons owning shares in a profitable company may look for some return on their investment in the form of a periodic dividend on their shares. This is usually paid yearly or half-yearly and the amount will depend on what the directors consider is available out of the profits of the company for distribution in this way. This can apply particularly where some of the shareholders are not directors and therefore draw no remuneration from the company; otherwise it is not uncommon for family private companies not to pay any dividends at all.

If your company pays a dividend it is also required to make a payment of *advance corporation tax* (ACT) to the Revenue within certain time limits. The name derives from the fact that the company is entitled to offset payments of ACT against its liability to corporation tax on its profits, primarily those of the accounting period in which the dividend is paid. This set off may be subject to certain restrictions and to the extent that it cannot be fully used then, the surplus may be carried back for relief for a period of up to six years or carried forward indefinitely.

The purpose of the tax is to ensure that the dividend can be treated in the hands of the recipient as income which has already suffered tax. Thus when the shareholder receives his net dividend he is also regarded as being entitled to a 'tax credit' (equivalent to the corresponding ACT) which is taken into account in his own tax settlement. Currently, the rate of ACT is one third, corresponding to the basic rate of income tax fixed for 1990/91 at 25% on the 'gross equivalent, i.e. the dividend plus the tax credit; by the same token, this rate of ACT applied in 1989/90. The operation of this may be illustrated as follows.

Example

Norah Bone Ltd is a company specialising in the sale of canned dog food. In the year ended 31 March 1990 the company made taxable profits of £900,000; on 31 July 1989 it paid a dividend of £75,000 to its shareholders.

Its corporation tax position for the year would be:

	£
Profits chargeable to corporation tax	900,000
Corporation tax at 35%	315,000
Dividend paid	75,000
ACT thereon, at ⅓rd	25,000
(= 25% of £75,000 + £25,000)	

The company would actually account for its corporation tax liability in two parts.

	£
ACT due 14.10.89	25,000
Balance ('mainstream liability') due 1.1.91	290,000
	£315,000

If a shareholder received out of this dividend £7,500 he would be entitled to a tax credit of one third of £7,500 i.e. £2,500. If, because of other income, he is effectively liable to income tax at a rate of 40% on this income, he would have additional tax (known as 'excess liability') of £1,500 to pay for the tax year 1989–90, calculated as follows.

	£
'Gross equivalent' i.e. £7,500 + £2,500	10,000
Income tax thereon, at 40%	4,000
Less tax credit	2,500
	£1,500

This further tax would be due on 1 December 1990 or 30 days after the issue of the notice of assessment if this is later (see question 2).

On the other hand, if the shareholder was not liable to tax at all on this income, for example because it was a charity, then it could reclaim the whole of the tax credit of £2,500 from the Inland Revenue.

The question has referred only to *dividends*. However, there are other categories of payments in money or money's worth called *distributions* which are liable to ACT in the same way. In particular where shareholders take assets, e.g. stock in trade, out of the company at less than market value, the undervalue is taxed as if it were a dividend. A similar result follows where shareholders put assets into a company at an overvalue. Transfers between a company and its shareholders do therefore need to be looked at carefully with this aspect in mind.

Where a company receives a dividend (or distribution) from another UK company, it is *not* liable to any corporation tax on that dividend. However, it cannot use the tax credit that goes with that dividend, except against any liability to ACT on dividends that it in turn pays. A set off in this way does reduce the eventual amount available for credit against the company's corporation tax liability.

59 As a director and shareholder of a company, should I draw remuneration or dividends from the company?

When investment income was generally subject to higher rates of tax than earned income, the best practice was for an individual to draw remuneration from his company rather than dividends. However, that bias against investment income has disappeared and there are now a variety of factors which need to be taken into account. The most appropriate answer depends very much on the particular circumstances of the company and of the individuals concerned and no decision in this area should be taken without the benefit of proper professional advice.

However, here are some of the considerations that need to be borne in mind.

1 An individual, including from 6 April 1990 a married woman, may claim personal allowances, etc. against dividend income as well as against earned income (e.g. remuneration).

2 Pension scheme contributions can only be paid where there is a source of earned income, whether through a company scheme or a

personal pension scheme (see question 16).

3 No national insurance contributions are payable on dividends; this could represent a real saving as compared with the Class I contributions due by both the individual and the company in respect of remuneration (see question 17). On the other hand, there could be some loss of benefit if the full contributions are not kept up.

4 Remuneration is normally paid under PAYE, with the appropriate relief for allowances and deductions being given (see question 27) but with any liability to higher rate tax being collected at the same time.

Dividends are effectively paid out under deduction of basic rate tax only, leaving any higher rate tax to be collected from the recipient later, as described in question 58.

5 It is possible to pay remuneration in arrears, for example by way of a bonus, some time after the year end when the company's results for the year are known, and relate this back so as to rank as a further deduction against that year's profits, provided that the emoluments are paid over within nine months of the end of the year concerned; this period is extended to 18 months where that year began before 6 April 1989 and ended before 6 April 1990. Care needs to be taken in dealing with amounts that may have already been drawn by way of 'advances' in this situation, as under certain circumstances these can lead to further tax liabilities arising on the company or on the individual.

It is not possible to relate back a dividend payment in this way and the corresponding ACT has to be relieved primarily against corporation tax on the profits of the accounting period in which the dividend is paid.

6 Income tax withheld under PAYE and national insurance contributions have to be accounted for to the Revenue on a *monthly* basis. ACT has to be accounted for only every quarter.

7 Where a company has established a pattern of paying dividends, this could affect adversely any valuation that has to be agreed with the Inland Revenue on a transfer of its shares in connection with a tax planning scheme for its shareholders, so possibly leading to an increased charge to inheritance tax (see question 91).

8 To avoid any challenge by the Revenue as to its deductibility in the company's accounts, it is advisable to maintain remuneration at a reasonable level commensurate with the duties performed by the directors concerned.

In any event, whether money is drawn as remuneration or

dividend, it will be sensible to try to bring the company's rate of tax and your own together as near as possible. As explained in question 52, a company currently pays tax at a rate of between 25% and 35% depending on its level of profits. You start paying tax (after allowances and deductions) in 1990/91 at 25%; as shown in question 1, this rises to 40% for taxable income over £20,700.

If the company is incurring trading losses, there may be little point in paying out any remuneration, except to the extent necessary to enable the directors to use all their personal allowances; once these have been lost, they cannot be picked up in a later year.

Remember that where a company is making losses there may be restrictions under company law as to how much, if anything, may be paid out as dividends.

60 How can I provide my employees with a stake in the company in a tax efficient way?

An individual who works for a company which is successful or which he believes is going to be successful is often interested in acquiring an interest in that company and so participating in its success in the longer term. By the same token, the directors of the company may see this as a way of providing their employees with an added incentive to stay with the company and make their own contribution to its success. This may be difficult, particularly if the company is an unquoted one with no market for its shares.

Basically, it must be recognised that where an employee acquires shares in his employer company other than for their full price, this is in effect an addition to his remuneration and the 'benefit' that he acquires is to be taxed accordingly. Indeed, in certain circumstances the legislation goes further and aims to tax as earned income the subsequent appreciation in value of those shares.

However, there are certain arrangements sanctioned by the legislation which allow these provisions to be avoided and permit employees to acquire shares in their employer company on advantageous terms. The provisions are very complex and expert professional advice is essential; what follows is only a brief summary of the current law and practice in this area. It should be emphasised that all these schemes require the approval of the Inland Revenue which must be obtained in advance.

Profit related pay (PRP)

In 1987 a tax-based incentive was introduced whereby employees would be encouraged to take part of their remuneration ('PRP') by sharing in the company's profits. This operates so that one-half of PRP will be free of income tax up to the point where it forms 20% of an employee's pay or £4,000 per annum, whichever is lower. It has been estimated that a married man on average earnings should receive relief amounting to approximately £10 per week. PRP is subject to national insurance contributions in the usual way. All private sector employees are eligible to receive relief except controlling directors. The employer must register the PRP scheme with the Revenue before it comes into operation. The scheme must relate to an identifiable 'employment unit' which could be the whole business or a sub-unit of it.

Employers will generally be free to design their own schemes but certain basic qualifications will be required.
1 There will have to be a clear relationship between the PRP of the employment unit and its audited profits.
2 New recruits and part-timers may be excluded. Otherwise, at least 80% of the employees within the employment unit must be covered by the PRP scheme.
3 The scheme must run for at least a year.

Obviously, any decision to implement a PRP scheme has to be made by the employer, probably after consultation with his employees. It has been suggested that a scheme could be introduced into pay bargains instead of a conventional increase in pay, possibly involving the conversion of some existing pay into PRP. It may also be possible to include current profit sharing schemes, provided that the qualifications set out above can be met.

Detailed guidance notes are available from the Revenue on application to Profit Related Pay Office, Inland Revenue, St Mungo's Road, Cumbernauld, Glasgow G67 1YZ (tel: 0236 736121).

Profit sharing scheme

In this plan, the company allocates a percentage of its profits (which need not be fixed) to a trust specially set up for this purpose; this amount is tax deductible to the company. The trustees use the money to acquire shares in the company which they hold in trust for those employees who have agreed to join the scheme.

In due course an employee can ask for the shares to be transferred to him absolutely. Normally no transfer can be made in the first two years; thereafter income tax is chargeable on the original market value of the shares when they are transferred in the third and fourth years and on 75% of that value in the fifth year; thereafter no tax is payable. While the trustees hold the shares, any dividends are paid to the employees entitled to them.

Broadly, the scheme must be open to all full-time employees of the company and the amount that may be allocated to any employee each year is limited to the greater of £2,000 or 10% of his earnings (up to a maximum of £6,000).

Employee share ownership plan (ESOP)

The 1989 Finance Act introduced a further initiative designed to promote wider share ownership among employees. An ESOP is essentially an employee benefit trust which is linked to a share participation scheme. This trust would normally be financed by contributions (which under certain circumstances would be tax deductible) from the employing company and this money would be used to acquire shares in the company; the trust may also borrow from a third party for this purpose. The shares are then passed over to employees either directly or through a *profit sharing scheme* of the kind described above.

At the time of writing (March 1990) the concept had attracted little attention; certain changes were announced in the 1990 Budget which it is hoped will stimulate greater interest.

SAYE share option scheme

This requires an individual employee to take out an SAYE contract for a period of five years, of the kind described in question 23. At the same time he is granted an option to acquire shares in the company at a set price.

At the end of five or seven years, the employee can cash in the contract and use it to acquire shares in the company at the option price, or he can keep the money and not take up any shares at all.

There are no tax consequences on an individual when he is granted the option nor when he acquires the shares. On any subsequent disposal of the shares he is subject to CGT in the usual way and with the benefit of the normal reliefs (see question 65).

Generally, the scheme must be open to all employees (with a

few exceptions). The maximum level of contribution is at present fixed at £150 a month with the minimum normally set at £10 a month; this may be restricted if the employee is already a participant in other SAYE schemes.

Approved share option scheme

This scheme, introduced in 1984, is different to the schemes already described in two major respects.
1 The scheme need only be open to a limited number of employees, selected by the employer, instead of being required to be open to all (or virtually all) employees.
2 The limit on the value of the shares that may be acquired under such a scheme is set at a much higher level than that laid down for the other schemes. The maximum allowed by law is the greater of £100,000 or four times salary, although an individual scheme may provide a lower limit.

There are a number of conditions that need to be satisfied both by the company and the participants in the scheme; provided that these are met, then any gain arising to the employee on exercising an option which he had been granted is not normally taxable and only CGT is payable on the disposal of the shares acquired through the scheme.

This idea has generated considerable interest, enabling companies to provide selected employees with a major incentive, and a substantial number of schemes have been set up.

61 How can I attract outside investment into my company with the benefit of tax relief?

The *business expansion scheme* (BES) was first introduced in 1981 and substantially modified in 1983. The objective is to encourage private investors to put money into a company and obtain immediate *income tax relief* on that investment. The main features of the scheme are noted below.
1 Income tax relief is given at the individual's highest rate of tax, i.e. 40% in 1990/91.
2 The maximum amount that may be invested in any one tax year is £40,000. The lower limit is £500 unless the investment is through a BES fund (see point 8 below) when this limit is normally £2,000.

3 For investments made in the first half of the tax year (i.e. between 6 April and 5 October), the investor may carry back half the BES relief to the previous year up to a maximum of £5,000.

4 For shares issued after 1 May 1990 the relief is limited to £750,000 per company in any 12 month period (previously the limit was £500,000), except for companies in ship chartering or private rented housing (*assured tenancies*) where the limit is £5 million.

5 Investments may be in any unquoted company trading wholly or mainly in the UK which is engaged in manufacturing, service, construction, retail or wholesale distribution or in certain other specified activities (which are liable to change from year to year!) Certain activities are excluded, particularly those with substantial asset backing or otherwise low exposure to risk.

6 Relief is only on ordinary shares with no special rights which must represent new capital in the company and these must be held for at least five years. If the shares are disposed of earlier (other than on the liquidation of the company), the income tax relief already given is clawed back.

7 The investor must not (together with his 'associates' as defined) own more than 30% of the shares in the company, he must not be connected with the existing shareholders and he may not act as a *paid* director of the company.

8 To enable prospective investors to be linked up with qualifying companies, a number of *BES funds* have been set up. These collect subscriptions from the investors and invest them in suitable companies which the fund managers have investigated. The managers will continue to monitor the progress of the companies on behalf of the investors.

9 As mentioned in point **6**, the shares must be held for a minimum of five years. After that the investor may dispose of the shares; where these were issued after 18 March 1986 no CGT is payable on their first disposal. For shares issued earlier, CGT is charged only on the excess of the sale proceeds over original cost (i.e. before taking account of any income tax relief). This disposal could be by way of the company buying back the shares; this could be intended from the outset, provided that it was available to all holders of that class of shares.

● **62   When and why is a receiver or liquidator appointed to a company?**

Ever since man first began to trade there have been businesses which have failed, so this is not a new phenomenon, but must always be regarded as part and parcel of the element of risk in starting up a business.

If a business fails it is said to be *insolvent* but this is something which is not defined. It is not just a matter of liabilities over assets, so a certain amount of subjective judgement is necessary. It has been said that there appears to be nothing wrong in the fact that directors incur credit, when they know the company is not able to meet all its liabilities as they fall due, but what is most definitely wrong is if the directors continue to incur credit when it is clear the company will *never be able to satisfy its creditors.*

The main areas with regard to corporate failures are *receiverships* and *creditors' liquidations*; the latter may be either a voluntary liquidation or a compulsory liquidation. Either way there is normally a formal appointment of a person to take control of the assets and business of the company.

A *receiver* may be appointed by a major creditor, e.g. a bank, to protect the security of its outstanding debt. A receiver, on taking appointment, becomes the agent of the company but this does not suspend the directors of the company, although in practice it will curtail their powers. The appointment will not alter the beneficial ownership by the company itself of its assets or business.

Should the directors prove unable to maintain that the solvency criteria are met, steps must then be taken to commence formal liquidation proceedings. Normally these take the form of a creditors' *voluntary winding-up* which involves summoning a meeting of shareholders to pass a winding-up resolution. Not more than one day later a meeting of creditors must be held (called at the same time as the shareholders' meeting) and they should confirm the view of insolvency and appoint a liquidator. As an alternative to this, particularly if urgent action is required, the directors of the company may apply to the court for a *compulsory winding-up order*, which will probably be provisional and subject to a later confirmation. Proceedings started in this way tend to be more formal and a good deal slower in the long run. Occasionally, when a liquidation follows a receivership, sometimes it will be clear that the assets of a company may be negligible and if the company cannot find an individual willing to act as liquidator (because there is little likelihood of him being paid) the role of the liquidator will be undertaken by an officer of the Department of Trade.

It is important to remember that liquidations have different implications to receiverships. The latter may only be temporary interruptions in a company's business but the appointment of a liquidator initiates the dissolution of the company.

Insolvency law has been substantially amended and a number of changes have been made to various aspects of its operation. In particular, a simplified form of receivership under direction of the court, known as *administration*, has been introduced and may be appropriate in certain circumstances.

● 63 Are there any special tax considerations relating to groups of companies?

The decision whether to run a business through one company or through a group of companies is dependent upon many factors, not all concerned with taxation, but nevertheless there are taxation aspects to be considered. A company carrying on trading activities is subject to corporation tax, and if those activities are divided up between different companies, even if they are all part of a group, *each company is treated separately, with its own profits and therefore its own corporation tax liability*.

There is no charging of the group as a whole on its total profits, but there are a number of reliefs which apply where the group companies are resident in the UK.

1 Dividends paid to a parent company may be paid without advance corporation tax (see question 58).

2 Interest and other annual payments may be paid between group companies without deduction of income tax (see question 53).

3 A parent company may pass any surplus advance corporation tax down to a subsidiary which can then use it, subject to certain restrictions, against its own liabilities to corporation tax (see question 58).

4 Certain assets may be transferred within the group without incurring a liability to CGT (see question 57) or to a balancing charge (see question 38).

5 All the trades carried on by members of a group are treated as one trade for the purpose of rollover relief for CGT purposes (see question 79).

6 Trading losses and other deductions may be used on a current year basis by another member of the group by means of what is called 'group relief'.

There are different rules for each category of relief depending on whether the company is a 51% or 75% subsidiary of its parent; there are also special provisions relating to value added tax (VAT) (see question 100).

It should be noted that none of these arrangements apply to companies which are under the common control of the same individual shareholders without constituting a legal group. In this situation, it may well be worth considering whether there could be advantages in setting up a group structure for these companies.

64 Can I set up a company overseas and if so what would be the tax position?

There is a certain amount of freedom if you should wish to set up a company overseas; there is no general rule to say that the profits of an overseas company are to be treated as those of its parent company resident in the UK (as defined in question 52), so this would seem to give scope for tax planning. However, there are various provisions preventing the avoidance of UK tax by the use of overseas companies. These were substantially modified in 1988, redefining corporate *residence* for UK tax purposes (again see question 52); although the most stringent provisions previously applicable were then withdrawn the rules are still very restrictive and it is essential to obtain specialist professional advice if any transactions of this kind are contemplated.

There are also special provisions which apply to overseas companies controlled by UK residents and operating in low tax countries (the so-called 'tax havens'). Under these provisions a UK resident company could be charged to corporation tax on a proportion based on its interest in the overseas company's profits, assets, etc.

Non-resident companies are only liable to pay corporation tax if they are carrying on a trade through a branch or agency in the UK. In these circumstances, the company will pay tax on the branch's profits, including the following:
1 trading income from the branch;
2 income from property or rights held by the branch;
3 gains accruing from the disposal of assets of the branch or agency in the UK.

Capital gains realised by a non-resident company may be followed through to the shareholders. A non-resident company cannot be a member of a group of companies for UK tax purposes (see question 63).

In the same way as for individuals (see question 26), where income is taxed in both the UK and overseas, it is usually possible to obtain relief for the overseas direct tax by way of credit against the corresponding UK tax.

5 SOME YOU WIN – SOME YOU LOSE

CAPITAL GAINS TAX AND THE INDIVIDUAL

65 What is CGT? What are the rates and do I still pay CGT if my gains are not substantial? ●

Capital gains tax (CGT), first introduced on 6 April 1965, is a completely separate tax from income tax. The basis of charge to this tax can be stated as follows: *when a chargeable person disposes of a chargeable asset, either a chargeable gain or an allowable loss will arise.*

You are a *chargeable person* if, during a tax year (i.e. during a year ending on 5 April), you dispose of a *chargeable asset* and at any time during that year you are resident or ordinarily resident in the UK (see question 34). There are special rules if you are domiciled outside the UK (again see question 34); if this is the case you should seek further advice. If you die, all your chargeable assets will be treated as disposed of, but death is *not* an occasion of charge for CGT purposes.

Any form of property, in the widest sense, and whether situated in the UK or not, can be a *chargeable asset*.

In simple terms there is a *chargeable gain* if the proceeds you receive on disposal of an asset exceed the cost of the asset at the date it was acquired. Similarly, if the proceeds on disposal are less than the cost of the asset at acquisition, an *allowable loss* will arise.

The rules were substantially amended in 1982 and subsequently so as to recognise the effect of inflation. With effect from *6 April 1988*, the gain or loss on any asset which has been held since before 31 March 1982 is calculated by reference to *the original cost or the market value of the asset at 31 March 1982*, whichever gives the smaller gain or loss when compared with the sale proceeds. (This exercise is generally referred to as *rebasing to 31 March 1982*.)

There is also a further allowance (known as *indexation*) which is intended to take account of inflation since 31 March 1982. This operates by applying to the cost a factor representing the increase in the retail prices index (RPI) from the date of acquisition to the date of sale. Where the asset was already held at 31 March 1982 indexation is applied to the greater of the original cost or the market value at 31 March 1982 but only by reference to the increase in the index from that date.

Examples

		£
(1) Shares sold May 1989 (RPI 115.0)		33,000
Cost in January 1983 (RPI 82.61)		12,500
Unindexed gain		20,500
Indexation allowance		
$\dfrac{115.0 - 82.61}{82.61} \times £12,500$		4,901
Chargeable gain		£15,599

		£
(2) Shares sold May 1989 (RPI 115.0)		33,000
Cost in January 1981	£12,500	
Market value at 31 March 1982 (RPI 79.44)		15,500
Unindexed gain		17,500
Indexation allowance		
$\dfrac{115.0 - 79.44}{79.44} \times £15,500$		6,939
Chargeable gain		£10,561

		£
(3) Shares sold May 1989 (RPI 115.0)		33,000
Cost in January 1981		18,500
Market value at 31 March 1982 (RPI 79.44)	£15,500	
Unindexed gain		14,500
Indexation allowance		
$\dfrac{115.0 - 79.44}{79.44} \times £18,500$		8,281
Chargeable gain		£6,219

As regards disposals prior to 6 April 1988 of assets held at 31 March 1982, the initial deduction in arriving at the unindexed gain was always the original cost. On the other hand, indexation was applied to the greater of cost or market value at 31 March 1982.

Where the sale proceeds fall between original cost and market value at 31 March 1982 so as to give rise to a gain by comparison with one base and a loss by comparison with the other, the computation is treated as giving rise to neither gain nor loss.

For disposals on or after 6 April 1988, where the indexation allowance exceeds the unindexed gain the full allowance is given so giving rise to an allowable loss for CGT purposes; where the unindexed result is itself a loss, the indexation allowance may be added so as to increase that loss. For disposals prior to 6 April 1988, the indexation allowance was restricted to the amount of any unindexed gain so leaving a nil result; where there was an unindexed loss no indexation allowance was given.

To save taxpayers the trouble of maintaining records of original costs of assets, an election may be made to have all assets treated as revalued at 31 March 1982 and taking this as the only base for computing gains or losses on disposals of assets from 6 April 1988. This election must be made not later than two years after the end of the tax year in which the first *relevant disposal* took place. A 'relevant disposal' is of any chargeable asset, so the term applies not only to an asset which is clearly within the CGT net but could also include one such as your only or main residence which is normally exempt from CGT provided certain conditions are met (see question 69). On the other hand assets which are always exempt from CGT (such as those described in question 68) would not give rise to 'relevant disposals'.

For *companies* the operative date for the current mode of computation is 1 April 1988 instead of 6 April 1988 and disposals are all considered by reference to accounting periods not tax years (see also question 57).

Special rules apply to assets acquired before 6 April 1965 (see question 77).

A further deduction (only for individuals not companies) is the *annual exemption* which is applied to aggregate gains less losses. For 1990/91 this has been fixed at £5,000 for each of husband and wife; for 1989/90 the limit was £5,000 applied to husband's and wife's gains taken together.

For trusts the annual exemption is generally half that applicable to individuals, i.e. £2,500 in 1989/90 and 1990/91.

After these deductions have been applied, any chargeable gain remaining for an individual is charged to *capital gains tax*. For years up to and including 1987/88, for individuals this was at a flat rate of 30%; for subsequent tax years the gain is taxed as if it were income at the taxpayer's marginal rate, i.e. 25% or 40% as the case may be.

● **66 If I am married, how does this affect my capital gains position?**

Up to 5 April 1990, the rules concerning husband and wife were as follows.

1 Transfers of assets between spouses living together were regarded as made on a basis of *no gain*, *no loss*. (The exceptions to this were on death where there is full exemption from CGT and the transfer of trading stock to or from either spouse.)

2 The houses of husband and wife living together are dealt with in questions 69 and 70.

3 Capital gains and losses were calculated for each spouse separately; unrelieved losses of one were set against net gains of the other except where there was an election to the contrary, which had to be made before 6 July in the year following the end of the year of assessment.

4 The net gains and losses were assessed on the husband, except for the year of marriage when the wife was assessed as if she was a single person (unless the marriage took place on 6 April). If the tax remained unpaid by the husband the Inland Revenue could press for payment by the wife, up to the amount she would have had to pay if a separate assessment election was in force (see **5** below).

5 Either party to the marriage could claim for separate assessment for CGT if they made application before 6 July following the end of the year of assessment. There was the same time limit for revoking such an election. The total payable remained unchanged but the wife would have had an assessment on her own gains and she would therefore be liable to pay her own tax. (This corresponded to the arrangement for separate assessment for income tax purposes described in question 8.)

The annual exemption for CGT purposes (see question 65) applied as if it was divided between the spouses in proportion to their respective taxable amounts, or where those amounts were less than the exempt amount and there were losses brought forward from previous years, in such proportions as they agreed.

With effect from 6 April 1990, in parallel with the reform of income tax for husband and wife described in question 9, married couples are to be taxed independently on their capital gains, with separate set-off of allowable losses and separate annual exemptions. Nevertheless, the facility to transfer assets between spouses on a no gain, no loss basis, as described in **1** above, still applies and this does provide opportunities for tax planning by husband and wife – see question 10.

Children who are minors are entitled to their own exemption limits which gives scope for future reduction in a family's CGT burden if transfers of part of a family shareholding are made to the children at any early stage – if this should create a loss, refer to the rules on 'connected persons' mentioned in question 75. *It is essential that any such transfers to the children are clearly and indisputably for their benefit.*

67 Are there any expenses that I can claim for CGT purposes?

If you incur expenditure when acquiring or disposing of an asset this can be used to reduce the chargeable gain. Expenses which are allowable fall into the following categories.

1 Costs incidental to the acquisition: These may only be deducted if they are actually incurred by the person acquiring the asset. They must be incurred *wholly and exclusively* for the purpose of the acquisition; this would apply to fees, commission, costs of transfer, etc., together with advertising costs incurred in finding a seller.

2 Improvements: Again, the expenditure must be incurred *wholly and exclusively* in respect of the asset, this time to enhance its value. Such expenditure *must* be reflected in the state or nature of the asset at the time of its disposal.

3 Establishing rights to the asset: Expenditure is allowable if it is incurred *wholly and exclusively* for the purposes of establishing, preserving or defending your title to the asset. This is a very strict rule and operates narrowly.

4 Costs incidental to the disposal: These are defined in the same way as the costs of acquisition and cover legal fees and the cost of advertising to find a buyer. Costs reasonably incurred in establishing any necessary valuation for CGT purposes will also be allowed.

General investment advice and expenditure on financial journals are *not* allowable.

● 68 Are any assets exempt from this tax?

Gains arising on the disposal of certain assets, as set out below, are exempt from CGT; by the same token any loss arising on their disposal is not allowable for these purposes.

Chattels: These are assets which are tangible and moveable. They are exempt if the disposal proceeds are £6,000 or less. A marginal relief applies where the proceeds slightly exceed £6,000. (For years up to 1988/89 the limit was £3,000.) There are also special rules dealing with 'sets' of chattels.

Motor cars: These are not chargeable assets unless they are of a type not commonly used as a private vehicle and unsuitable to be so used.

National Savings Certificates, Premium Bonds, etc: These, and other government securities which are not transferable, are exempt whenever they are acquired or disposed of. Premium Bond winnings are also exempt.

Government securities ('gilt-edged'): These are exempt as regards disposals made on or after 2 July 1986; previously the exemption applied only if the stock had been held for more than 12 months. A similar exemption applies to certain *fixed interest loan stocks* issued by companies after 13 March 1984; while gains on these are exempt from CGT, losses incurred on or after 14 March 1989 will be allowable for these purposes.

Betting and other winnings: Betting winnings are not chargeable gains and rights to winnings obtained by any pool betting or lottery are not chargeable assets.

Foreign currency: Exempt when disposed of providing it was acquired only for personal and family expenditure.

Medals and decorations: Exempt unless acquired by purchase.

Compensation for damages: Exempt if received for personal or professional wrong or injury; if the damages, etc., relate to an asset, payment will constitute a disposal.

Life assurance policies and deferred annuities: Exempt when disposed of or realised by the original policyholder but *not* when disposed of or realised by another person who acquired them by purchase.

69 Is my home a chargeable asset?

In general, if your dwelling-house is your only or main residence throughout your *period of ownership* there will be no charge to CGT when you sell the property: this exemption extends to the building and (in most cases) up to one acre of land.

However, you may at some time during your period of ownership be required to live elsewhere, through the terms of your employment for instance, or a period of working abroad, in which case your claim that the house is exempt could be affected. The following periods of absence (i.e. the time you are *not living* in your house) do *not* affect your claim, providing you live in the house for a period both before and after (except for points **4** and **5**) the specified periods of absence.

1 In any circumstances, a period, or periods, not exceeding three years in all.

2 A period during which you are employed abroad.

3 A period, or periods, not exceeding four years in all during which you are prevented from living in the house by reason of the location of your work or a condition by your employer requiring you to live elsewhere.

4 The first 12 months of ownership prior to taking up residence during which the house is being built or alterations made.

5 The last two years of ownership, regardless of whether or not you are living there.

The periods of absence mentioned are also ignored where husband and wife are living together and the conditions are satisfied by the spouse who is not the owner.

Where the conditions for exemption from CGT are not satisfied throughout the period of ownership, the gain is apportioned on a time basis to arrive at the amount which is chargeable.

If as a result of a breakdown of marriage, one spouse ceases to occupy the matrimonial home and later transfers it to the other spouse who has continued in occupation, no gain will be chargeable.

Where you are living in 'job-related accommodation' in the circumstances described in question 21, the house which you are buying for your own use may also rank for exemption from CGT as described above.

70   What is my position if I own more than one property?

You are only allowed to have one dwelling house at a time for the purposes of the exemption referred to in question 69. If you have more than one house available for your residence at the same time you may elect which one is to be treated as your main residence. A chargeable gain will arise on the disposal of the other property and you should therefore seek advice regarding the value of each – this way it may be that the smaller of the gains arising will be charged to tax by electing for the property giving rise to the larger gain to be exempted as your main residence. Notice of the election must be given to the Inspector of Taxes not later than two years after the date that it is to take effect and will continue until varied by further notice. If you do not make a choice the Inspector of Taxes will make it for you: if you disagree with his decision you have the right to appeal with a view to enabling the matter to be settled formally; this follows the procedure described in question 3. If you acquire a dwelling house for the sole purpose of selling it again at a profit there will be no exemption from CGT, even though you may live in it for a period; to go further, if you make several transactions of this kind, the Inspector may seek to charge income tax on the profits instead of CGT, thus excluding any entitlement to indexation or the annual exemption (see question 65), on the basis that you are 'trading'.

Up to 5 April 1988 if the property is used as the residence of a dependent relative of yourself or your spouse and he or she occupies the house rent-free, this property will be exempt from CGT *in addition* to your own main residence. Relief must be claimed from the Inspector of Taxes and is given in proportion to the part of the period of ownership during which the property is occupied by the relative. Note that this exemption can only apply to *one* dependent relative per marriage (or per claimant, if he or she is single). The relief will no longer apply for disposals of property on or after 6 April 1988 except in relation to a home which would have qualified for relief on a disposal before that date. (See question 20 for possible mortgage interest relief implications.)

There is also an exemption from CGT that may be available if you are the owner of a property as the personal representative or trustee of a *deceased person*. There are special rules applicable here and if you consider this may apply to you, you should seek professional advice.

71 Does it make any difference if I let my house or take paying guests?

You may wish to supplement your income in a tax year by taking a lodger into your home; if he lives with you as part of your family, sharing the living accommodation and taking meals with you, this will *not* affect the exemption for CGT when you sell the property.

If, however, you let part of your home to a tenant, depending on how much of the home is let (i.e. how many rooms, etc.) and for how long, the exemption may be restricted. Relief is allowed on the let portion of the house but this must not exceed the amount of exemption due on the rest of the house. This relief is only given up to a maximum of £20,000 in any case.

72 What is the position if I use part of my house as an office?

If you are employed on the basis that you are required to work at home, you may be able to claim an income tax allowance for the use of a room in your home as an office (see question 20). Similarly, if you are self-employed you may also be able to claim that you have to use part of your home as an office. If part of your house is used *exclusively* for business purposes you may lose the exemption from CGT on that part of the house. You should therefore take care *not* to set aside part of your home exclusively as an office – *be sure that the room you use is also used for private purposes*.

● **73 Are gifts chargeable to CGT?**

A gift of an asset is a disposal for CGT purposes; however, if you are making a gift there are obviously no sale proceeds, so the chargeable gain is computed by substituting (for sale proceeds) the *market value of the gift* at the date it was given. For these purposes the market value is the price which the asset might reasonably be expected to fetch if it were sold on the open market.

There are certain gifts which are altogether *exempt* from CGT:

1 transfers between husband and wife where they are living together (see also question 66);

2 gifts of cash in sterling;

3 gifts to charities;

4 gifts of land, buildings and chattels to the National Trust and other similar bodies, and of works of art, etc. for the national benefit.

It should also be noted that *there is no CGT charge arising on an individual's death.* Although this event is treated as a disposal of his assets at their then market value, it may give rise to a charge to inheritance tax (IHT) as described in Chapter 6.

● **74 If I make a gift which is not exempt from CGT, is there any relief that I can claim?**

If the gift is not exempt as described in question 73, the chargeable gain arising (as if the asset had been sold at its market value) is taxed on the donor (the person making the gift) in the normal way. However, for gifts made prior to 14 March 1989, it was possible, provided that the donee (the recipient of the gift) was an individual resident in the UK, to *hold over* the gain. This meant that the gain that would otherwise arise was deducted from the donee's acquisition value (i.e. the market value at the date of the gift) so that there was no longer any chargeable gain arising to the donor. The donee would pay the tax deferred in this way when he came to dispose of the asset (subject to any exemptions that he might then be able to claim) as he would have a lower acquisition value to deduct from his sale proceeds leaving a higher chargeable gain to arise then. Both the donor and donee must elect jointly for this relief to apply and the election must be made to the Inspector of Taxes within six years of the end of the tax year in which the gift was made.

If the donee ceases to be resident in the UK within six years from the end of the tax year in which the gift was made and he still holds the asset, the holdover liability becomes immediately payable by the donee. If they cannot get the tax from the donee the Inland Revenue can pursue the donor for it instead.

For gifts made on or after 14 March 1989, the general holdover relief is withdrawn and it is now only available in certain limited circumstances, as follows:

1 Gifts of assets used in a trade, profession or vocation carried on by the donor.

2 Gifts of shares in a trading company (or the holding company of a group of trading companies), provided that one of the following tests is satisfied:

(a) the shares are not quoted on a recognised stock exchange or on the Unlisted Securities Market;

(b) the donor is an individual, the shares are quoted and the company is his *family company*. This requires that *either* the donor is able to exercise at least 25% of the voting rights attaching to the shares in the company *or* he is able to exercise at least 5% of those rights and he with members of his family can exercise more than 50%. (For this purpose, 'family' means spouse, and your own and your spouse's brother, sister, ancestor or lineal descendant.)
If the underlying assets are not all 'chargeable business assets' (i.e. used in the trade carried on by the company or in the group), there may be some restriction to the relief that may be attributed to the shares, so that only a proportion of the gain arising on the shares may be deferred and the balance becomes immediately taxable in the normal way;

(c) the donor is a trustee who is able to exercise 25% of the voting rights relating to the shares in the company.

3 Gifts of heritage property, as in question 73 point **4**.

4 Gifts to political parties.

5 Gifts upon which there is an immediate charge to inheritance tax, for example gifts into discretionary trusts or to companies

113

where the provisions relating to *potentially exempt transfers* (see question 82) do not apply.

6 Gifts of land (or sales at below market value) to a non-charitable registered housing association (see question 88 regarding inheritance tax exemption of such transfers).

● 75 If I make a capital loss, can I turn this to my advantage?

You will no doubt have realised by now that it is to your advantage to keep your chargeable gains below the exemption limit mentioned in question 65. The treatment of losses incurred in both the current and previous years can play an important part in reducing your chargeable gains to this figure.

Losses realised in the current year must be set off against gains for the current year as far as it is possible to do so and any excess may then be carried forward. However, *losses brought forward* from a previous year need only be set off against current year gains to the extent necessary to reduce those gains to the annual exemption limit (see question 65). The benefit of this is twofold, as you are still able to carry any excess losses forward but you have also been able to utilise the tax-free exemption limit.

Losses brought forward from previous years are therefore of importance, and if you are approaching the end of a tax year with no realised gains it may be possible to create losses by *bed and breakfast transactions* (see question 76) to build up a bank of losses to carry forward to future years. *A word of warning:* if you have already realised gains in the current year, 'bed and breakfast' transactions to create losses should only be carried out in order to take the gains below the taxable threshold, as any current year losses to the extent that they reduce the gains below the exemption level will be wasted.

As a general rule you cannot set your capital losses against your other income and if you are in business you cannot set trading losses against capital gains. However, it is possible to claim the set-off of a loss arising on the disposal of shares in an *unquoted* trading company against your other income for income tax purposes *provided* that the shares were acquired by subscription in cash or money's worth and not brought from a previous shareholder. The shares must *never* have been quoted on the Stock Exchange and there are other tests to be satisfied before the relief is given.

Another general rule concerning losses is that they may not be carried back to be set against gains of an earlier year; there is an exception to this in the year of death when losses can be carried back for three years, covering the later gains first.

If you make a disposal of an asset to a *connected person* and incur a loss, that loss may only be utilised against gains arising from future disposals to the same person, if he or she is still 'connected' with you. As an individual you are 'connected' with any relative of yourself or your spouse and the spouse of any of those relatives. If you are a trustee you are 'connected' with the settlor and any other person or body corporate connected with the settlement. If you are in partnership you are 'connected' with each partner and their respective spouses and relatives. Finally, a company is 'connected' with any of its shareholders or with any other company in the same ownership.

There may also be loss relief available in respect of a *qualifying loan* – see question 79.

76 What is a 'bed and breakfast' transaction?

Generally, *bed and breakfast* transactions relate to quoted stocks and shares, i.e. those dealt in on a recognised stock exchange, which are sold on one day and repurchased through the stock exchange on the following day (or later). This arrangement provides a means of crystallising an accrued gain up to the level of the annual exemption (see question 65). There will then be no tax to pay on the realised gain but the shares will now have a higher 'cost' for CGT purposes on a subsequent sale.

Example
Shares which cost £8,000 in 1983 were worth £12,500 in February 1990. If they had then been sold and repurchased the following day, the chargeable gain (ignoring costs and indexation allowance) would have been £4,500; if there were no other CGT gains in 1989/90, this would be covered by the annual exemption and so there would be no tax to pay. The 'cost' of the shares would now be £12,500 and this would be used in relation to any future disposal.

The same idea can also be used to crystallise accrued losses where these can be set against other realised gains so as to reduce the tax then chargeable. It will be appreciated that this reduces the ongoing 'cost' of the shares concerned and so may only be a deferral of the tax saved.

It is essential that a genuine sale is made through the market and that the repurchase is also genuinely made through the market at least one business day later; otherwise the Revenue will match the two deals and the object of the exercise will have been lost.

It should be noted that stamp duty and stockbrokers' charges will be due on these transactions; these should be allowable as described in question 67. In the example given, these might amount to £250; it may be as well to agree these with the broker beforehand.

77 I have assets which I acquired before CGT was introduced on 6 April 1965. What is the position on these?

CGT was introduced on 6 April 1965 and a fundamental principle brought in at that time was that you should not be taxed on any gain arising *before that date*. With the passage of time and the introduction of rebasing to 31 March 1982 (see question 65) this question is likely to be academic in most cases. However, it may still be important where the so-called *time apportionment basis* applied at 6 April 1965.

This basis applies to virtually all assets held at that time, with the exception of quoted stocks and shares and of land with development value, and proceeds on the assumption that the sale proceeds less the original cost gave rise to an overall gain which was deemed to have arisen evenly over the period of ownership. That overall gain is then apportioned to and from 6 April 1965; the latter proportion is then compared with the unindexed gain or loss (see the examples in question 65) and the lesser amount taken before applying the indexation allowance. (If the asset was acquired before 6 April 1945 the gain is calculated as if the acquisition was made on that date but still using original cost.)

In the case of *quoted stocks and shares*, the alternative base to the 31 March 1982 value is either the original cost prior to 6 April 1965 or the market value at that latter date, as quoted on the relevant stock exchange, whichever would give the smaller gain or smaller loss. This would then be compared with the gain or loss arising by reference to the 31 March 1982 value as before.

So far as *land with development value* (defined as land showing a greater value than that which would be appropriate in its current use only) is concerned, the alternative base of its value at 6 April 1965 *must* be used instead of original cost.

78 What are 'paper for paper' transactions and how do they affect my capital gains tax position?

If you hold shares in a public company you may have realised that some transactions do not involve the actual buying and selling of shares. For instance, the company may decide not to distribute its profits as dividends, but to capitalise part of them (perhaps to build up reserves), in which case there may be a *bonus issue* of additional shares to the existing shareholders for which they pay nothing. On the other hand, a company seeking to increase its capital by an issue of new shares may allocate some of the new shares at a preferential price to its existing shareholders. This is referred to as a *rights issue*. In the *reorganisation of a company's capital*, blocks of shares may be exchanged or two companies may *amalgamate* or *merge* (or one company may *take over* another) by the exchange of share capital. In none of these situations are you buying shares for cash in the normal way.

For the purposes of CGT, if you acquire shares in any of the above circumstances, this is not classed as a chargeable occasion. The new or increased holding is, on the occasion of a later disposal, treated as having been acquired at the same time and at the same cost (plus any payments made for 'rights' issues) as the original holding.

In some instances you will be given the new shares automatically (e.g. 'bonus' issue), but with a 'rights' issue you are able to make a choice as to whether or not you take up the new shares. If you decide not to take up the offer you may then 'sell the rights' to the new shares for a (usually) relatively small consideration. This is a chargeable occasion, but if the amount you receive does not exceed 5% of the market value (on that day) of the shares you already hold there will be no charge to CGT at that time. The amount received is deducted from the acquisition cost of the holding, thus increasing the gain on an eventual disposal.

If the transaction offered by a company means you receive a capital distribution in money or money's worth (possibly in addition to the shares offered) which is not treated as income, you are then treated as having disposed of a part interest in the shares you hold and a gain is then calculated using only a proportion of the acquisition cost as the base cost for this purpose.

● 79 Are there any other reliefs for which I may qualify in certain circumstances?

The following few brief notes concerning other reliefs are not a comprehensive guide. The rules are complicated and if you consider that you may qualify for relief under any of these headings you should seek further advice.

Rollover relief: A trader disposing of assets used exclusively for the purpose of his trade, *who applies the sale proceeds in purchasing other assets to be used for a trade*, may elect to defer CGT by deducting the amount of the chargeable gain arising on the sale of the old asset from the acquisition cost of the new asset. The purchase of the new asset must take place within one year before, or three years after, the disposal of the old asset, though these time limits may be extended at the Revenue's discretion.

If only part of the sale proceeds is used to purchase the new asset there is a corresponding loss of relief. Furthermore, this relief is only given on any gain remaining when *retirement relief* (see below) has been taken into account.

Retirement relief: This relief applies where the individual is over 60 years of age (or has to retire earlier through ill-health) and disposes of whole or part of a business which is owned by him or of shares and securities in his family trading company; for this purpose a 'family' company requires that the individual retiring *either* is able to exercise at least 25% of the voting rights attaching to the shares in the company *or* he is able to exercise at least 5% of those rights and he with his relatives can exercise more than 50%. (For this purpose, 'relatives' means spouse and your own and your spouse's brother, sister, ancestor or lineal descendant.)

There are many conditions to be satisfied relating to the transaction and past history of the business or family company concerned; if these are fulfilled throughout a maximum qualifying period of ten years, relief will be given to its full extent. For periods of less than ten years a proportionate reduction is made, on a time basis, so that the minimum 'relevant percentage' is 10%, based on a minimum period of one year. Furthermore, relief is given if, in association with a sale of shares in his family company, the inidividual also disposes of an asset owned by himself that has been used by the company – again, there are various conditions to be fulfilled.

For disposals on or after 6 April 1988, the relief gives full exemption on £125,000 plus half the gains between £125,000 and £500,000. In all cases the relief is given against the part of the gain relating to *chargeable business assets* and the relief is then subject to the percentage reduction mentioned above.

Qualifying loan loss relief: First of all, it must be established what constitutes a *qualifying loan*.

The loan must have been given, after 11 April 1978, to a resident of the UK for use wholly in his trade (so that the borrower may also be a company), profession or vocation. The provisions do not apply to borrowings in the form of loan stock or any other similar marketable security; losses on these may be claimed in the normal way.

Provided that the Inspector of Taxes is satisfied that the claimant and the borrower were not spouses living together or companies in the same group, and that the lender has not assigned his right of recovery, loss relief may be allowed to the extent that part of the capital element of the loan has become irrecoverable. If at a later date following a loss claim, all or part of the sum is recovered, a chargeable gain will arise on the claimant.

80 When do I pay my CGT and are there any other administrative details I should know?

CGT becomes due and payable by individuals on *1 December following the end of the year of assessment* to which the gains relate, or 30 days after the issue of the notice of assessment, whichever is later. It is therefore possible to make a disposal on say 6 April 1990 on which the CGT will not be due until 1 December 1991 at the earliest.

If you disagree with the assessment you have the same right to appeal as for income tax (see question 3) and the same provisions also apply to a request for postponement of the tax charged, interest on unpaid tax and payment of a supplement on tax repayable (see question 5).

Where the consideration to be paid in respect of an asset you have sold is paid to you by instalments, it is possible for you to *pay tax by instalments* over a period not exceeding eight years, if you can satisfy the Revenue that to pay the tax in one sum would cause you hardship.

Finally, do not think that if the Revenue does not know of the gains you have made you will not have to pay the tax; the Revenue has its own way of tracing property transactions and share dealings. You must notify the Revenue of your gains when you complete your income tax return and there are *penalties for failure to do so* – see question 6.

6 CAPITAL WAYS OF SAVING TAX

INHERITANCE TAX

81 What is inheritance tax (IHT)?

Assets passing at death have been subject to various forms of taxation since *estate duty* was introduced in 1894. Estate duty only taxed assets passing on death and certain lifetime gifts, but CGT also applied on death between 1965 and 1971.

In 1974 *capital transfer tax* was introduced as a wide ranging tax on gifts made during lifetime and on assets passing on death on a cumulative basis. Special provisions were also brought in to tax transactions using trusts and settlements in various ways.

In 1986, a number of radical changes were introduced to the scheme, including a change of name to *inheritance tax* (IHT). The tax now applies generally to assets passing on *death* and to *gifts made within seven years before death*. Certain other categories of lifetime gifts may also be subject to the tax and these are considered in questions 82 and 83.

The rate of tax charged depends on the aggregate value of the assets passing on death, or on gift where there is an immediate charge to IHT (see question 82), together with the cumulative value of transfers made in the preceding seven years. For transfers made on or after 6 April 1990 no tax is charged on the first £128,000 of that aggregate value; the excess is taxed at a flat 40%. For transfers made between 6 April 1989 and 5 April 1990 (both dates inclusive) the threshold was £118,000, with the excess again taxed at 40%.

Gifts made up to seven years before the death are included with assets passing upon death at their value at the date of the gift, but using the rates of tax in force at the date of death. However, only gifts made up to *three years* before the death have to be included in full; for gifts made earlier, a form of tapering relief is available so that only a proportion of the full charge will apply. The table below shows the relevant details.

Years between gift and death	Proportion of full charge %
3–4	80
4–5	60
5–6	40
6–7	20

82 Are any lifetime gifts affected by IHT?

In general, for gifts made on or after 18 March 1986 other than those made within seven years before the death of the donor, there will be no lifetime charge to tax:
1 on gifts between individuals;
2 on gifts into accumulation and maintenance trusts (see question 93) or into trusts for the disabled;
3 on gifts made into interest in possession trusts (i.e. those where an individual has an entitlement to income) on or after 17 March 1987.

These are generally referred to as *potentially exempt transfers*.

However, subject to the exceptions described in question 88, a charge will be made on gifts at any time into other forms of trust. The rates applicable will be half those set out in question 81.

83 Are certain types of gift subject to special treatment?

So far we have assumed that a 'gift' is what it says it is, namely a free and unencumbered transfer of an asset.

However, special rules apply where the gift is not made outright: technically this is referred to as a *gift with reservation* and would apply where the donor continues to enjoy some benefit from the gifted asset. A simple example of this would be where an individual gives his house to another member of the family, subject to him (the donor) having the right to go on living in it rent-free. In such a case, the gift is treated as being made at the time (although in many cases the gift will come within the terms of a potentially exempt transfer, so that no tax will then arise; see question 82). Nevertheless the value of the gift is retained in the donor's estate and he is treated as making a second gift when the reservation is released or the enjoyment finally ceases. In the example of the house already mentioned, this could apply when the donor moved out to live elsewhere giving up his rights of occupation, or perhaps on his death. If the gift is thereby treated as taking place on the donor's death or within a period of seven years before, IHT will apply as described in question 81.

84 How are husband and wife treated for IHT?

Unlike income tax and CGT, husband and wife are treated as separate individuals for IHT purposes.

Furthermore, a transfer between husband and wife is generally exempt from the tax with one exception. Where the spouse receiving the gift is domiciled outside the UK (see question 85), only the first £55,000 will be exempt; any balance may therefore come within the 'seven year' charge (see question 81).

Where one spouse has substantial assets and the other has not, it may be worthwhile reducing the possible exposure to tax on death by topping up the smaller estate so that each can obtain the maximum benefit of the nil rate band.

85 How is IHT affected by my domicile?

If you are *domiciled* in the UK (see question 34) you will be liable to pay IHT on all your assets irrespective of where they are situated. If you are domiciled abroad tax is still payable, but only on any assets you have situated in the UK. The meaning of domicile is discussed in general terms in question 34 but this is modified for IHT purposes as follows:

1 An individual is deemed domiciled in the UK for IHT purposes if he has been resident in the UK (see question 34) in 17 out of the last 20 tax years including the one in which the death or gift took place (thus it is possible for an individual to be caught if he has been in the UK for no more than 16 years and one day).

2 An individual who goes abroad on a permanent basis so as to become accepted as no longer domiciled in the UK in the normal way will continue to be treated as domiciled here for IHT purposes for a further three years.

86 When is the tax payable and who is responsible for paying it?

Tax is due within six months of the end of the month in which the death occurred, and interest, currently set at 11%, runs from that date. Different rules apply in relation to those lifetime gifts which are chargeable to tax.

The persons primarily responsible for paying the tax are the *personal representatives*, but the Inland Revenue do have power to follow the liability through to any person in whom the property passing is vested after death. In the case of a lifetime gift which is caught, the tax attributable to that gift is normally collectible from the recipient unless there is a special provision in the donor's will allowing it to be charged against his estate.

Where any tax has already been paid on a gift, for example under the previous rules applicable to capital transfer tax, this will be allowed as a credit against the corresponding tax arising on the death.

87 What are the alternatives if I do not have the necessary funds available to pay the tax?

If the necessary funds to pay the tax are not available, the Revenue may accept any of the following property as a payment in kind: land, buildings and contents associated with those buildings; pictures, prints, books, manuscripts, works of art, scientific objects or other items, or collections of such items, should they be of national, scientific, historic or artistic interest.

88 Can I make gifts which are not chargeable to IHT?

There are certain categories of *lifetime transfers* which are not chargeable to tax; these reliefs do not apply on death.

Annual exemption: The first £3,000 of transfers each tax year is exempt and unused relief may be carried forward for one year only against transfers in excess of the limit for the following year. Unless there is a regular pattern of making gifts, so that these take place at least every other year, the benefit of this exemption may be lost.

'**Small' gifts:** The first £250 of transfers to any one individual in each tax year is exempt in addition to the annual exemption mentioned above. Unused relief cannot be used in a later year. The exemption applies only to outright gifts, not to settlements. It is therefore possible to pay any number of people up to £250 each in a year and still be outside the scope of IHT altogether. However, the relief cannot be used to cover the first slice of a larger gift; thus a transfer of £1,000 could be covered by the annual exemption, leaving £2,000, but not covered by the £250 small gifts exemption so as to use only £750 of the annual exemption.

Marriage gifts: Transfers made in consideration of marriage are exempt, but only within set limits which vary according to the degree of affinity between the transferor and the parties to the marriage. If the transferor is a parent of one of the parties to the marriage, he may give £5,000; if the transferor is a more remote ancestor he may give £2,500; if the transferor is one of the parties to the marriage the limit is £2,500; anyone else may give £1,000.

For this exemption it is important to ensure that there is evidence that the gift is actually made in consideration of the marriage and it should be completed *before* the marriage.

Normal expenditure out of income: If a transfer is effected out of income it may not be relevant to IHT. To qualify for this exemption, the Revenue must be satisfied as to the following three conditions:
1 The transfer is made as part of the normal expenditure of the transferor.
2 The transfer is made out of his income (comparing one year with another).
3 After allowing for all such transfers the transferor is left with sufficient income to maintain his usual standard of living.

The expenditure must be 'habitual' and the Revenue will look for a pattern of payments made to the same person. The expenditure must involve cash outlay; gifts of assets will only qualify if they were bought for the purposes of making the gift. 'Income' is taken as net of income tax for these purposes.

The following transfers are exempt from tax both as lifetime gifts and on death.

Charities: Transfers to charities and to charitable trusts (see question 93) are wholly exempt from IHT.

Political parties: If you should wish to make a donation to a *qualifying* political party, this will be exempt from IHT. But prior to March 1988 transfers in excess of £100,000 made on death or within 12 months prior to death were taxable.

A political party only 'qualifies' if it has two MPs or if it has one MP and gained at least 150,000 votes at the last General Election.

Gifts to housing associations: On and after 14 March 1989 a gift of land (or its sale at below market value) to a non-charitable registered housing association is exempt from IHT (see question 74 regarding the corresponding capital gains tax holdover relief).

National heritage: There are three different exemptions in this category, viz. gifts for national purposes, gifts for public benefit and conditional exemption.

It is essential that specialist professional advice is taken in connection with any possible claim for relief under these provisions.

1 *Gifts for national purposes:* The transfer is exempt if it becomes the property of a specified body – certain museums, galleries, and trust funds are specified by name (e.g. the National Trust); similar national institutions may be approved by the Treasury; many museums and art galleries maintained by local authorities and government departments are also eligible.

2 *Gifts for public benefit:* The transfer is exempt if the asset which then becomes the property of a non-profit making organisation, provided the Treasury gives its consent. The property so transferred may be land, buildings, works of art, etc., and the Treasury will be looking for items of outstanding scenic, historic, scientific, architectural or aesthetic value, as appropriate. The Treasury usually requires undertakings to be given to preserve the asset and to provide reasonable access to the public and the exemption may be lost if these undertakings are breached.

3 *Conditional exemption:* The property involved in this relief is basically the same as for gifts for the public benefit (see point **2** above). The transfer is conditionally exempt to the extent that it is attributable to property designated by the Treasury. The property remains in private ownership and the Treasury will require certain undertakings to be given, particularly public access, before the exemption is allowed. Again, IHT becomes payable if there is a

breach in the conditions or if the property is sold, unless the
undertakings are renewed.

89 What is excluded property?

Excluded property is not included in an individual's estate either
for the purpose of lifetime transfers or in the event of his death.
Excluded property includes the following:

1 Property situated outside the UK if the beneficial owner is
domiciled abroad as recognised for IHT purposes (see questions
34 and 85).

2 A reversionary interest (i.e. something which reverts to you)
providing it was *not* purchased by you.

3 Certain government securities beneficially owned by persons not
domiciled or habitually resident in the UK (see questions 34 and
85).

4 National Savings owned by persons domiciled in the Channel
Islands or the Isle of Man.

5 Property passing as a result of death on active service.

6 Cash options under approved annuity schemes.

7 Overseas pensions.

8 Property owned by members of visiting armed forces.

It should be particularly noted that an individual's private residence is *not* excluded from the charge to IHT so that there is no
exemption corresponding to that applicable for CGT (see questions 69 and 70).

90 If I have made transfers chargeable to IHT, are there any reliefs I can claim?

The following gives a few brief notes with regard to reliefs which
may be available if you have transferred a particular form of
property, or the circumstances are unusual. This is *not* a comprehensive guide and if you consider you may be eligible for any of
these reliefs you should seek further specialist advice.

Business property relief: Basically this relief provides that if you
transfer *relevant business property* the value transferred will be
reduced by a percentage which will vary depending on the type of

business property concerned. The relief can be claimed whether the transfer is made during lifetime or at death and there is no limit to the value transferred which may qualify for this relief. 'Relevant business property' includes:

• a business or interest in a business (reduction 50%);

• shares/securities in a company which was controlled by the transferor immediately before the transfer (reduction 50%);

• non-controlling shareholdings of more than 25% in a company where the shares are not quoted on a recognised stock exchange or the Unlisted Securities Market (reduction 50%);

• other non-controlling shareholdings in a company not quoted on a recognised stock exchange or the Unlisted Securities Market (reduction 30%);

• in certain circumstances, land, buildings, machinery and plant used for business purposes (reduction 30%).

There are various conditions that must be satisfied before the property is eligible for relief.

Agricultural property relief: This relief applies to transfers made during your lifetime or at death and provides that if the value transferred is attributable to the agricultural value of agricultural property in the UK, and the property is owned by a working farmer, the value may be reduced by 50% of the agricultural value.

Where the land is let to a working farmer, for transfers made after 15 March 1983 the landlord may claim a reduction of 30% of the agricultural value.

This relief is subject to various tests as to ownership and occupation on death and where relevant on transfer within seven years before death.

Relief for woodlands: A claim can be made that the value of trees or underwood growing on land in the UK (which is not agricultural property) be left out of account in determining the value transferred on the owner's death. Relief is to be claimed, by the person who would be liable to pay the tax, within two years following the death, but this time limit may be extended. The basic condition to be satisfied is that the woodlands must have been owned by the deceased for five years prior to his death or have been acquired by gift or inheritance. There will be no charge to tax unless the woodlands are disposed of either by sale or gift so it is possible to extend the relief through a succession of deaths.

Voidable transfer: Inheritance tax is repayable in respect of any transfer which is subsequently declared void by operation of law, e.g. on bankruptcy.

91 How is my estate valued at my death?

Your estate at death includes all the property of whatever description to which you were beneficially entitled. Exceptionally life assurance policies are included in the estate at their full value. At death your estate will generally also include property contained in a settlement if you had a vested interest in the capital or income of it.

For many forms of property, the value will be an obvious amount or relatively easy to calculate, but problems occur when valuing *unquoted shares* because a hypothetical situation must be assumed – this involves a hypothetical sale in a hypothetical open market between a vendor and purchaser both of whom are also hypothetical! This principle for valuing unquoted shares has been refined over many years and it is now well established that the larger the holding in general the greater the price per share that it should command. In certain circumstances adjustments may be made to the open market value in arriving at the amounts for IHT and CGT purposes, so that there may be material differences between the valuations applied to the two taxes.

Shares beneficially owned by either husband or wife, or by any trust in which either spouse has a vested interest in the income or capital, or by any charity as the result of a gift made by either spouse after 15 April 1976, are *related property* for IHT (but not CGT) purposes. Any related property is then treated as a single holding for valuing any transfer made by the husband or wife. It follows, therefore, that although the separate shareholdings of husband or wife may only be minority holdings, when taken together they may constitute a majority holding, and it is as part of the latter that the IHT valuation must be considered.

Similar considerations apply where a valuation is required of assets acquired in a lifetime transfer.

92 Is it possible to change arrangements made by a will after death has taken place, and if so, what are the tax consequences?

It is possible to change arrangements made by a will by what is called a *deed of family arrangement* which effectively permits a deceased person's will to be rewritten after his death and any tax will then be calculated as if the original will had been written in the same terms as the deed. For IHT and CGT purposes the change is effective from the date of death, but for income tax purposes it is only effective from the date of the deed.

To be effective for tax purposes, the deed must be entered into within two years of death, by an instrument in writing, and the persons doing so must notify the Inland Revenue within six months thereafter. The point of making such a deed would seem to be lost if additional tax became payable, but if this is the case (perhaps because the new arrangements have been set up for other than tax reasons), the persons liable to pay the additional liability (i.e. primarily the personal representatives) must be included with the persons joining in the agreement.

All persons who may benefit under the original will must agree to the making of a deed of family arrangement if it affects their interests. This may not be feasible where the interests, even quite remote, of infant beneficiaries are involved. It is essential to obtain expert legal advice on the feasibility of entering into such arrangements.

Proposals were brought in on the 1989 Finance Bill for the removal of this particular tax arrangement and there was considerable discussion on the point. In the event the government withdrew their proposals totally but indicated that this area was still under review and that further proposals for amendment might be proposed in due course.

93 Are there any special provisions relating to settlements?

The use of settlements and trusts as a form of tax planning has always attracted considerable attention from the legislators and settlements of all kinds are specially treated for IHT purposes. This is a highly complex area and what follows is only a brief summary of the current position.

Apart from the trusts mentioned in question 82 and those described below, tax is charged at half the normal rate on any gifts made into a settlement at any time.

Where the trust has an *interest in possession* (broadly there is a person entitled to receive the income of the trust), the assets of the trust will be treated as if they were part of that person's estate for the purpose of determining the tax payable on his death.

Where the trust is what is called *discretionary*, so that there is no one entitled to any specified part of the income or capital of the trust, a special charge to tax at reduced rates is levied on the assets of the trust every ten years or when any assets are transferred out, for example to a beneficiary.

Special treatment is given to the following types of settlement.

Accumulation and maintenance trust: The following conditions *must* be met:
1 One or more persons will become entitled to an interest in possession (which may be absolute or need only be an interest in the income) on or before attaining the age of 25.
2 Income is accumulated unless used for the maintenance, education or benefit of a beneficiary.
3 Not more than 25 years have elapsed since the creation of the settlement *or* all the beneficiaries are grandchildren of a common grandparent.

If the trust qualifies, no tax will arise on gifts made into it more than seven years before the settlor's death, the periodic charge mentioned above for discretionary trusts will not be payable and no further tax will arise when a beneficiary attains his interest.

Protective trust: This arrangement is intended to protect the assets in trust against the ravages of a profligate beneficiary: in particular it could come into operation where the beneficiary attempts to assign his interest to someone else. This would give the trustees discretion over the income so that the trust would become 'discretionary' as defined above but the periodic charge already referred to would not be payable even on the subsequent death of the beneficiary.

Trust for the mentally disabled: There is no tax payable if the trust is created for a mentally disabled person more than seven years before the donor's death, and the periodic charge is deferred until the death of the mentally handicapped person.

Charitable trust: A trust which is wholly charitable is not subject to a tax on entry and it is exempt from the periodic charge and from tax on all distributions.

131

Capital Ways of Saving Tax

Employee trust: A trust of this type may qualify for deferment of tax where the beneficiaries are restricted to persons of a class defined by reference to employment, persons married to those so defined or charities. Payments to beneficiaries are not classed as capital distributions and the periodic charge is deferred until a capital distribution payment is made.

7 THE INDIRECT TAX YOU MUST PAY

VALUE ADDED TAX

94 How does value added tax (VAT) operate?

VAT is a wide ranging form of indirect tax which has an impact on most forms of business operation in the UK. Currently the tax applies to *all* supplies of goods and services made in the course of a business. The tax is presently charged at a single rate of 15%.

A *taxable person* (see question 95) is required to charge tax (called *output tax*) on all supplies (with certain exceptions, see question 96) made by him to his customers and account for this tax, normally on a quarterly basis, to HM Customs and Excise (C & E) for it. Against this liability, the taxable person is entitled to take credit, subject to certain restrictions, for tax on supplies of goods and services made to him *for business purposes* (called *input tax*) during the same accounting period (but see question 97).

Normally, output tax has to be included in a trader's VAT return on the basis of invoices *issued*, not necessarily paid for. Similarly, input tax is claimed on the basis of invoices *received*. However, it is permissible for traders having a turnover of less than £250,000 a year (excluding VAT) to elect to go onto a cash accounting basis. This means that a business will only have to account to C & E for VAT when it has actually *collected* the tax from its customers; it will thereby get immediate relief for bad debts which is otherwise available only after two years' delay. By the same token, input tax could only be claimed as the bills were actually paid.

It is also possible for traders having a turnover of less than £250,000 a year (again excluding VAT) to opt to make their VAT returns once a year instead of quarterly. The trader will be required to make nine monthly payments on an estimated basis during the year concerned and pay the balance with his return two months after the end of the year.

Where a trader suffers more input tax in a period than the output tax he has to account for, C & E will repay the excess.

However, where a business does not make any taxable supplies, either because its turnover is not sufficient for it to be registered for VAT (see question 95) or because all its supplies are *exempt* from VAT (see question 96), it is not entitled to any credit for input tax, as described above. If a business has a mixture of taxable and exempt supplies, as defined for VAT purposes, some restriction may be applied to the amount of input tax for which it can claim credit. This is looked at further in question 97.

● 95 What are the rules regarding registration for VAT?

One of the most important features of VAT is registration: VAT is to be accounted for by *taxable persons* who make *taxable supplies* of goods and services in the UK, during the course or furtherance of their business. A *taxable person* is someone who makes or intends to make taxable supplies while he is *registered* or required to be *registered*. The point at which you are liable to be registered is governed by various turnover limits, but if you are an 'intending trader' you may still register voluntarily, provided that you can satisfy C & E that you are carrying on a business and that you do intend to make taxable supplies in the course or furtherance of that business.

If you have just started in business the date or point at which you should register is clearly important. Output tax can be an unexpected expense but perhaps even more important, if you are not registered for VAT purposes, you cannot reclaim the input tax you have paid on goods and services supplied to you; this could be most important in the earliest days of your business before you are obliged to register for VAT purposes, although under certain circumstances it may be possible to reclaim tax on goods or services supplied prior to registration. The turnover level must be kept under review; currently the limit for registration purposes is £25,400 per annum.

Prior to 21 March 1990, the registration requirements were more stringent, in that the trader was required not only to monitor his turnover in the past 12 months (the previous limit for this was £23,600) but also each quarter (where a limit of £8,000 applied); in addition if the trader anticipated that his turnover would exceed the annual limit (£23,600) in the next 12 months, he was required to register. Now, registration based on future turnover is only required if the annual limit (£25,400) is expected to be exceeded *in the next 30 days*.

If the turnover of your business is below the limits mentioned, you can still register on a voluntary basis where you are making taxable supplies by way of business. This could be helpful where a small business might find itself at a competitive disadvantage compared with VAT-registered businesses. C & E have made it clear that such voluntary registration will only be considered where the business concerned represents a substantial part of the trader's livelihood and refusal of registration would cause a significant amount of input tax to be irrecoverable.

If, at the end of a quarter, your turnover exceeds the limit, you will be required to register unless it is accepted by C & E that the annual limit will not be exceeded; tax will then be chargeable from the end of that quarter. Failure to get this right can result in a great deal of unnecessary expense – if at any time C & E think the annual limit might be reached you will be required to register immediately and tax may be assessed from an earlier date.

Remember that the onus is on you as the trader to notify C & E that you should be registered for VAT.

You should also be aware that C & E have stringent powers of enforcement in connection with VAT, particularly in relation to registration and to the timely and accurate completion of VAT returns. Penalties for failure to comply with all these requirements can be substantial. See question 98.

After you have registered for VAT purposes, if there is any change in your circumstances you *must* inform your local VAT office and there are penalties for failure to do so. Many of the possible changes which could occur will require the *deregistration* of your business, which must be notified to the VAT office within ten days of the change. The most important circumstances are as follows:

1 The business is closed down or sold.

2 The proprietor of the business takes one or more persons into partnership.

3 A partnership ceases to exist but one of the former partners becomes the sole proprietor of the business.

4 A company is incorporated to take over a business previously carried on by a sole proprietor or partnership.

5 A business previously carried on by a company is taken over by a sole proprietor or partnership.

6 Taxable supplies cease for some other reason.

A business may apply to deregister for VAT purposes, but is not compelled to do so, if its annual turnover is expected to fall below £22,600. From 1 June 1990, the limit for deregistration is raised to £24,400.

When your registration is cancelled you may be awaiting either tax invoices for services already provided to you or the completion of services relating to the business you carried on when you were registered. If so, you may not be able to claim input tax on these services on your final VAT return, but you may be able to claim a special repayment subsequently.

Other changes in circumstances may be dealt with by a simple amendment to your registration (e.g. address, change in the trading name of the business, etc.).

● 96 What exceptions are there to the VAT standard rate charge?

For a variety of social and political reasons, each country that operates a VAT system deems it appropriate that certain supplies should not be subject to VAT. The UK is no exception to this procedure and indeed it has currently the widest range of exclusions from VAT of any country in Europe.

Exclusions from the charge to VAT operate in two ways: zero rating and exemption.

Zero rating

In this case, the supplier concerned is treated as being subject to VAT at a nil rate, but otherwise regarded as being taxable. There is therefore no effect on the supplier's entitlement to reclaim input tax (see questions 94 and 97).

The more important zero rated supplies at present are as follows:
- exports of goods;
- food excluding restaurant meals and catering supplies;
- books, newspapers and other publications;
- the supply of fuel and power, water and sewerage services (from 1 July 1990, only for domestic purposes);
- construction of buildings for use as dwellings or for certain residential or charitable purposes;
- certain international services;
- public transport;
- certain supplies to and by charities;

– clothing and footwear for children or for protective purposes.

The detailed conditions under which these supplies are exonerated from VAT are complex and specialist advice may need to be taken in any specific situation.

Exemption

Supplies in this category are regarded as not being subject to VAT. Any supplies made to the business which are attributable to such exempt supplies do not rank at all for input tax credit as described in question 94.

The more significant exempt supplies are as follows:
– sale or letting of land (with certain exceptions);
– insurance services;
– betting, gaming and lotteries;
– most financial services;
– education as provided at school or university;
– health and medical services;
– burial and cremation.

Again the detailed conditions relating to this relief are complex and specialist advice is essential in situations of difficulty.

97 In what circumstances could my entitlement to reclaim VAT be restricted?

There are two major situations where a registered trader may not be able to recover the whole of the input tax charged on goods and services supplied to him.

Non-deductible inputs

The VAT suffered on certain inputs is specifically defined as being non-deductible, so that it does not rank for credit under any circumstances. The expenses presently within this exclusion are as follows.

1 Purchase of motor cars (except by motor traders) but not commercial vehicles. The exclusion does not apply to hiring or leasing charges nor to running costs.

2 Entertainment and hospitality, other than (reasonably) for staff.

3 Expenditure by a builder on fixtures and fittings of a kind that would not normally be installed by him.

4 (With effect from the date that the 1990 Finance Act becomes law, say end July 1990), expenses incurred by a business in providing domestic accommodation for *directors* and their families. This restriction may also be extended to apply to other employees at a later date, after due consultation.

5 Expenditure other than for business purposes.

Partial exemption

As indicated in question 94, some restriction of input tax may be applicable where a business has a mixture of taxable (including zero rated) and exempt supplies. Many businesses are regularly in this situation, for example those in the property, construction or financial services fields. However, many other businesses, normally fully taxable, could find themselves treated as partly exempt by reason of the sale of a property or the receipt of rent or of bank deposit interest.

A fundamental principle of VAT is that input tax attributable to exempt outputs should not be recoverable. Where there is a mixture of taxable and exempt outputs, the input tax borne by the business has to be apportioned between those categories of output on a reasonable basis. This apportionment is operated on the following basis:

1 Input tax on goods and services wholly used or to be used in making taxable (i.e. standard rated and zero rated) supplies is recoverable in full.

2 Input tax on goods and services wholly used or to be used in making exempt supplies or in carrying on any non-taxable activity cannot be recovered.

3 The remaining ('residual') input tax is recoverable only to the extent that the goods and services on which it is incurred are used in making taxable supplies.

There are no specific rules laid down for ascertaining the input tax recoverable under **3** and a business may do this in any way it prefers. While the business is not generally required to seek prior approval from the local VAT office for any calculation it adopts it may be prudent to do so.

A further complication, which took effect on 1 April 1990, is that where a partly exempt business invests in certain categories of *capital goods*, the amount of input tax that may be recovered in relation to such expenditure is to be adjusted over a subsequent period to take account of changes in the input tax restriction in that period. This applies to the following items: computers and computer equipment worth £50,000 or more: the adjustment period is five years; land and buildings (or parts of buildings) worth £250,000 or more: here the adjustment period is 10 years.

There are also various rules under which 'incidental' and *de minimis* amounts may be ignored for these purposes, so enabling input tax to be recovered in full.

It should be noted that C & E are altogether more strict in the application of these provisions than they may have been in the past and it is essential for any business in this situation to take professional advice as to any arrangements that it can make to minimise its exposure to tax.

98 What are the penalties for failing to comply with the VAT regime?

Following a major investigation into the regulatory powers of both the Inland Revenue and Customs & Excise, substantially more stringent penalty provisions have now been introduced in relation to VAT. The more significant penalties are described below:

Late registration: Where a person fails to register in circumstances where he should have registered, he is liable to a penalty based on the tax that would have been charged had he taken the necessary steps to notify C & E of his liability to register, as follows:

- belatedness not exceeding nine months – 10%
- belatedness exceeding nine months but not exceeding 18 months – 20%
- belatedness exceeding 18 months – 30%

In any event there is a minimum penalty of £50.

Default surcharge: A VAT return and any payment due with it is normally required to be *received* by C & E by the end of the month following the end of the accounting period. Where this deadline is not met either because C & E have not received the return or they have received the return but not the payment due, the trader is regarded as being in default.

Repeated failures to comply can lead to a *default surcharge* being levied in accordance with the following procedure:

1 Where there are two defaults within a year, C & E may issue a surcharge liability notice, which remains in force for a year from the end of the period relating to the second default;

2 If, within the period of the surcharge liability notice, there is a further default, the trader is liable to a surcharge of 5% of the tax due for that period or £30 if greater;

3 In addition the surcharge period is extended for a further year from the date of the later default and so on for each subsequent default;

4 For each subsequent default during the surcharge period (as extended), the surcharge will be increased by 5% up to a maximum of 30% (or £30 if greater);

5 Only where the trader has not been in default for a year will the surcharge liability notice lapse.

It has been held that it is crucial to the preservation of a taxpayer's rights that he does receive the surcharge liability notice described in **1**; it is a good defence if the taxpayer can establish that he did not receive the notice and can be used to rebut a contention that proof of posting constitutes proof of delivery.

At present, these provisions are not being applied to regular repayment traders. However, in other cases, a return which is late which shows a refund due to the trader will still be counted as being in default although no surcharge will be applied; this could affect the amount of surcharge applicable to subsequent defaults.

Serious misdeclaration penalty: With effect from 1 April 1990, a penalty will be charged where there is an understatement of tax due, or an overstatement of an entitlement to a repayment of tax, on a VAT return.

These provisions are also to apply in circumstances where an assessment to VAT issued by C & E understates the true liability and the taxpayer makes no attempt to draw the error to C & E's attention.

Where these circumstances apply, the trader will be liable to a penalty equal to 30% of the tax which could have been lost; this is after giving due allowance for any understatement of input tax or overstatement of output tax made for the period concerned.

The penalty will only apply where the tax lost either:

(a) equals or exceeds 30% of the true amount of the tax due for the period, or

(b) equals or exceeds whichever is the greater of £10,000 and 5% of the tax due for the period.

Looking at this in terms of numbers, a penalty of 30% of the

amount underdeclared will apply in any of the following situations:
1 where the true tax liability in the period of account is £33,333 or less and the underdeclaration equals or exceeds 30% of that liability;
2 where the true tax liability in the period of account is between £33,333 and £200,000 and the underdeclaration exceeds £10,000;
3 where the true tax liability in the period of account exceeds £200,000 and the underdeclaration exceeds 5% of that liability.

In principle, this new penalty regime will involve notifying the VAT office each time an error is found. However, to make it easier to deal with minor errors, businesses will be able to include amounts of up to £1,000 in total in their periodic VAT account. These will be treated as tax due in the period in which they are returned.

Unauthorised issue of tax invoices: Where a person issues a document which purports to be a tax invoice at a time when he was not in fact registered for VAT, he is liable to a penalty of 30% of the tax included on that invoice or, if greater, £50 regardless of the number of invoices involved.

Defence against penalty charges: In each of the penalty situations described above, the trader may put forward a defence of *reasonable excuse* for the default concerned. However, the legislation does specifically exclude the following from providing a 'reasonable excuse':

(i)   insufficiency of funds;
(ii) reliance on another person or dilatoriness or inaccuracy on that person's part.

Where C & E are not prepared to accept an explanation as providing a reasonable excuse, the trader may take the matter before his local VAT tribunal, which hears initial appeals on VAT disputes generally.

In relation to the defence of reasonable excuse as it may apply to a failure to notify registration, C & E have published guidelines showing circumstances where there might be a 'reasonable excuse' for late registration:

1 Compassionate circumstances: Where the individual trader is totally responsible for running a small business and he or a member of his immediate family was seriously ill or recovering from such an illness at the time notification was required.

2 **Transfer of a business as a going concern:** Where the trader has taken over a business as a going concern and there was little or no break in trading activity and he has forwarded returns and paid tax on time under the previous owner's registration number.

3 **Doubt about liability of supplies:** Where there is written evidence of an enquiry to C & E about the liability of supplies and that liability has remained in doubt.

4 **Uncertainty about employment status:** Where there are genuine doubts as to whether the individual concerned is self-employed or employed, or where he can produce correspondence with the Inland Revenue about these doubts.

5 **Effective date of registration earlier than required:** Where the trader has asked for registration at an earlier date than that which was legally required in the belief that this was necessary in order to reclaim tax on stocks and assets of the business. C & E have indicated that this excuse could only apply if there was no reason to believe that the trader's taxable turnover would exceed the annual threshold with effect from the requested date.

C & E have also indicated that, in reliance on a number of decisions of the VAT tribunals, they are not prepared to accept any of the following as providing a 'reasonable excuse' in this context:

(a) the trader's ignorance of the law or his misunderstanding of the registration requirements, e.g. because of lack of trading experience;

(b) the trader's oversight of the need to register, e.g. because of business pressures;

(c) the trader's difficulty in forecasting his annual turnover, e.g. because of delay in preparing his annual accounts;

(d) some oversight or misunderstanding between the partners or directors of the business;

(e) an error in calculating annual turnover;

(f) a claim that some earlier notification of liability to register was made to C & E though there is no evidence that it was pursued further. It should be noted that C & E claim to record all registration enquiries;

(g) there is no loss of tax because all the trader's customers are themselves registered and therefore entitled to reclaim as input tax any VAT charged;

(h) there was no intent on the trader's part to evade the payment of tax;

(i) the severity of the possible penalty or other mitigating circumstances.

Although the maxim 'ignorance of the law is no excuse' still prevails, it does appear that VAT tribunals are concerned to find mitigating circumstances wherever they reasonably can to support a claim of 'reasonable excuse' for late registration. Traders in this situation should look closely at the circumstances of their particular situation to see whether a defence along those lines can be put forward; a well prepared and carefully documented case must also be helpful here. The following are some of the points of general application that have emerged from the many cases taken on the point:

* Many cases have been fought, not on whether a reasonable excuse would be available in certain circumstances, but on whether those circumstances exist. The availability of records and other evidence is often crucial.
* Evidence that C & E have been kept informed, and their instructions followed, can be particularly helpful in establishing a reasonable defence. This may also serve to provide some protection in respect of the tax itself (likely to be even more important in serious misdeclaration cases).
* Each case is considered by the tribunal on its own particular facts. Often factors which might not in themselves provide a reasonable excuse will be seen as establishing one when taken together.

99 Are there any situations where the VAT treatment needs to be specially considered?

There are a number of situations where, although there is no actual sale ('output' in the VAT jargon), tax has to be accounted for to C & E as if there had been one. The most notable of these are the following:

1 Where goods are supplied for non-business purposes, for example, for the private use of the proprietor of the business or of an employee.

2 Where goods are supplied by way of gift, even though for business purposes, and their cost is more than £10 (this includes a series of gifts of less than this amount to the same person where the total cost exceeds £10).

3 Where petrol, supplied by the business, is used for private motoring by the proprietor or employees of the business. This is based on the scale of charges used for income tax purposes (see question 31), as follows:

Engine size	Quarterly scale £	Monthly scale £
Up to 1400cc	120(15.65)	40(5.22)
1400–2000cc	150(19.56)	50(6.52)
Over 2000cc	225(29.34)	75(9.78)

The amount of VAT is shown in brackets. The scale charges are reduced by 50% where the business mileage exceeds 4,500 a quarter (or 1,500 a month where monthly returns are made).

It should be emphasised that, unlike the income tax charge which applied only to directors and 'higher-paid' employees (as defined in question 30), this charge applies to private petrol supplied to *all* employees and also to the proprietor of a business and to the partners in a partnership.

● 100 Is there any way I can plan to minimise the tax charge?

It is important that the VAT significance of transactions which the business intends to carry through is correctly understood, as any mistakes may be difficult to rectify after the event and can be expensive.

The actual format of your accounting records can give rise to planning considerations, for example, in the case of dealers in certain categories of second-hand goods, such as motor cars or works of art, where C & E regulations are strict but there can be definite advantages in making use of them. Similarly retailers who deal mainly in cash, and who do not normally issue tax invoices, have the choice of a number of schemes which are aimed at arriving at a calculated figure for output tax. If you are a retailer it is clearly important that you select the scheme most beneficial to you, so you should always take professional advice when setting up in such business.

As the implications of VAT accounting are more connected with cash flow, if you are a trader who regularly claims a repayment you may apply to make a monthly return rather than the normal quarterly return.

If your business is a company which is a member of a group of companies it may be beneficial to be registered as a group and not as separate companies. These arrangements can operate very flexibly in practice and can provide useful savings in administrative expenses and on occasion in irrecoverable VAT costs.

8 THE RANGE OF POSSIBILITIES

● **101 A final word**

The present government is committed to encouraging investment in business and to assist industries and areas where there are special problems. The new *enterprise initiative* promoted by the Department of Trade and Industry (DTI) is being widely publicised to ensure that everyone is aware of what schemes and assistance may be available.

The DTI, under this scheme, has committed £80 million in 1989/90 and £63 million in 1990/91 to help businesses obtain the advice and support of experienced advisers. Any independent business (whether in manufacturing or services) with less than 500 employees may apply for assistance. Normally the level of support will be half the cost of a five to 15 man day consultancy project. In the *assisted areas* this support is increased to two-thirds of the cost. The assistance may also include free advice, for up to two days, by an experienced enterprise counsellor.

In addition the following support is also available:

1 In the *assisted areas* and the *urban programme areas*, selective assistance for projects which are commercially viable, create or safeguard employment, demonstrate a need for assistance and offer a distinct regional and national benefit.

2 In the *development areas*, independent firms with fewer than 25 employees may apply for
– *investment grants* of 15% of the cost of fixed assets up to a maximum grant of £15,000;
– *innovation grants* of 50% of the agreed cost of a specific project up to a maximum grant of £25,000.

3 Advice on the development of *overseas markets*.

4 A wide range of training is available to help meet the needs of small businesses and their employees.

Further information on these arrangements is available from any regional office of the DTI.

Another measure, the *loan guarantee scheme*, was devised to help people to start in business. The Department of Employment, in conjunction with a number of banks and other financial institutions, will provide guarantees of up to 70% (85% in certain inner city areas) of loans over two to seven years on approved ventures up to a maximum of (currently) £100,000. Interest is charged at a commercial rate with an additional premium of 2½% payable to the Department on the guaranteed proportion of the loan. Since it was introduced the scheme has covered lending of over £700 million to more than 21,000 small firms.

At a lower level, the Manpower Services Commission operates a scheme (known as the *enterprise allowance scheme*) which sets out to assist unemployed people who wish to start their own business. The scheme is designed to assist people who would otherwise be deterred by paying an allowance of £40 a week for up to 52 weeks as a supplement to their business receipts while they are becoming established; a recipient must put up at least £1,000 from his own resources. Free business counselling is also available. The allowance is subject to tax and national insurance as for other self-employed earnings but it is not subject to the multiple charge on such earnings which normally applies in the opening years of a business (see question 36).

You will by now have realised that the title of this book is not altogether true; the ways of saving tax are *not* limited to 101, for there are endless possibilities to be considered. Indeed, if you were to count the reliefs, allowances, pieces of advice and so on given in these 100 answers you would find they totalled well in excess of 101! However, you must remember that this book cannot supply you with *all* the answers – it can only draw your attention to matters to which more detailed care and attention should be given. Always seek professional advice on any taxation or other financial matter about which you are not clear.

APPENDIX 2
PERSONAL ALLOWANCES 1989/90 and 1990/91

	1990/91 £	1989/90 £
Personal:		
single person	3,005	2,785
married man	–	4,375
married couple's	1,720	–
Wife's earned income (maximum)	–	2,785
Age (see Note 1):		
age 65–75		
single person	3,670	3,400
married man	–	5,385
married couple's	2,145	–
age over 75		
single person	3,820	3,540
married man	–	5,565
married couple's	2,185	–
Widow's bereavement allowance	1,720	1,590
Additional allowance for widows and others in respect of qualifying children	1,720	1,590
Blind person (available to each qualifying spouse)	1,080	540
Life assurance (see Note 2):		
given by deduction at source	12½%	12½%

Notes

1 Excess over personal allowance withdrawn by £1 for every £2 of income over £12,300 (1989/90: £11,400).

2 Relief given only on policies in force on 13 March 1984. No relief allowed on policies entered into after that date.

APPENDIX 3
BENEFITS IN KIND – CARS AND CAR PETROL
1989/90 and 1990/91

	Under 4 years old £	Cars 4 years old or more £	Car fuel £
1990/91			
Cars with original market value up to £19,250 and having a cylinder capacity:			
1400 cc or less	1,700	1,150	480
1401 cc–2000 cc	2,200	1,500	600
more than 2000 cc	3,550	2,350	900
Cars with original market value up to £19,250 and not having a cylinder capacity: original market value			
less than £6,000	1,700	1,150	480
£6,000–£8,499	2,200	1,500	600
£8,500–£19,249	3,550	2,350	900
Cars with original market value of £19,250 or over:			
£19,250–£29,000	4,600	3,100	900
over £29,000	7,400	4,900	900
1989/90			
Cars with original market value up to £19,250 and having a cylinder capacity:			
1400 cc or less	1,400	950	480
1401 cc–2000 cc	1,850	1,250	600
more than 2000 cc	2,950	1,950	900
Cars with original market value up to £19,250 and not having a cylinder capacity: original market value			
less than £6,000	1,400	950	480
£6,000–£8,499	1,850	1,250	600
£8,500–£19,249	2,950	1,950	900
Cars with original market value of £19,250 or over:			
£19,250–£29,000	3,850	2,600	900
over £29,000	6,150	4,100	900

APPENDIX 3 (continued)
BENEFITS IN KIND – CARS AND CAR PETROL
1989/90 and 1990/91

Notes

1 Where there is preponderant business use (i.e. more than 18,000 business miles a year), both the car and car fuel benefits are reduced by half.

2 Where the car has only insubstantial business use (i.e. less than 2,500 business miles a year) or it is an additional car provided by the employer, the car benefit is increased by a half. There is no increase in the car fuel benefit.

3 Where two members of a family are both employees of the same employer, each is charged in respect of his own car. It has been made clear that, notwithstanding the family relationship, there is to be only one charge in respect of each car.

4 Where a single car is shared by two employees of the same employer, there is only a single charge, apportioned between them as appropriate.

5 Where the car is not available for a period of time (normally at least 30 consecutive days in a year), both the car and car fuel benefits are reduced proportionately.

6 The car fuel benefits only apply to cars made available by the employer; the normal benefit-in-kind legislation (see question 30) applies where petrol is provided by an employer for an individual's own car, hire car, etc.

7 The car fuel scales are also to be used to assess VAT on fuel used for private journeys by registered traders and their employees (see question 99).

APPENDIX 4
NATIONAL INSURANCE CONTRIBUTIONS
1989/90 AND 1990/91

	Employees	*Employers*
1990/91		
Class 1: employed (see Note 1)		
Not contracted out – *on all earnings*		
up to £45.99	Nil	Nil
up to £79.99	2% on first	5%
up to £124.99	£46 + 9% on	7%
up to £174.99	remainder up	9%
up to £349.99	to £350	10.45%
over £350	no further charge	10.45%

Classes 2 and 4: self-employed	
Class 2 fixed per week	£4.55
no liability if earnings below £2,600 p.a.	
Class 4 earnings related	
on profits between £5,450 and £18,200	6.3%
(see Note 3)	

Class 3: non-employed	
Voluntary rate per week	£4.45

APPENDIX 4 (continued)
NATIONAL INSURANCE CONTRIBUTIONS
1989/90 AND 1990/91

	Employees	*Employers*
1989/90		
Class 1: employed 6.10.89 to 5.4.90		
(see Notes 1 and 2)		
Not contracted out – *on all earnings*		
up to £42.99	Nil	Nil
up to £74.99	2% on first	5%
up to £114.99	£43 + 9% on	7%
up to £164.99	remainder up	9%
up to £324.99	to £325	10.45%
over £325	no further charge	10.45%

Classes 2 and 4: self-employed

Class 2 fixed per week	£4.25
no liability if earnings below £2,350 p.a.	
Class 4 earnings related	
on profits between £5,050 and £16,900	6.3%
(see Note 3)	

Class 3: non-employed

Voluntary rate per week	£4.15

Notes

1 Reduced rates of Class 1 contributions, for both employers and employees, are applicable in respect of *contracted out employees* on earnings between £46 and £350 per week in 1990/91 (1989/90: £43 and £325).

2 A different scale applied to Class 1 employees' contributions for the period 6 April to 5 October 1989.

3 Half the Class 4 (earnings related) contributions are allowable as a deduction from the individual's total income for income tax purposes.

APPENDIX 5
INHERITANCE TAX RATES 1989/90 AND 1990/91

The following rates apply on death:

Transfer made on or after 6.4.90		*Transfer made between 6.4.89 and 5.4.90*	
Rate	*Band*	*Rate*	*Band*
%	*£*	*%*	*£*
Nil	1–128,000	Nil	1–118,000
40	over 128,000	40	over 118,000

Certain lifetime gifts to which an immediate change applies, are taxed at half the above rates (see question 82).